A Course of Advanced Lessons in Clairvoyance and Occult Powers

A Course of Advanced Lessons in Clairvoyance and Occult Powers

Swami Panchadasi (Villiam Valker Atkinson)

ISBN: 978-93-5128-511-3

First Published in 1916
Indian Reprint in 2017

Published by

Kalpaz Publications
C-30, Satyawati Nagar,
Delhi – 110052
E-mail: kalpaz@hotmail.com
Website: kalpazpublications.com
Ph.: +91-9212142040

Cataloging in Publication Data—DK
Courtesy: D.K. Agencies (P) Ltd. <docinfo@dkagencies.com>

Panchadasi, *Swami,* 1862-1932, **author.**
A course of advanced lessons in clairvoyance and occult powers / Swami Panchadasi.
pages cm
"First published in 1916"—Title page verso.
ISBN 9789351285113

1. Clairvoyance. 2. Telepathy. 3. Astral projection. I. Title.

BF1325.P36 2017 DDC 133.84 23

SYNOPSIS OF THE LESSONS

LESSON - I

The skeptical person who "believes only the evidence of his senses." The man who has much to say about "horse sense." "Common Sense" versus Uncommon Senses. The ordinary five senses are not the only senses. The ordinary senses are not as infallible as many think them. Illusions of the five physical senses. What is back of the organs of physical sense. All senses an evolution of the sense of feeling. How the mind receives the report of the senses. The Real Knower behind the senses. What the unfolding of new senses means to man. The super-physical senses. The Astral Senses. Man has seven physical senses, instead of merely five. Each physical sense has its astral sense counterpart. What the astral senses are. Sensing on the astral plane. How the mind functions on the astral plane, by means of the astral senses. The unfolding of the Astral Senses opens up a new world of experience to man.

LESSON - II

The two extra physical senses of man. The extra sense of "the presence of other living things." The "telepathic sense." How man may sense the presence of other living things apart from the operation of his ordinary five physical senses. This power is strongly developed in savages and barbarians, but has become atrophied in most civilized men, by continued disuse. It is now vestigal in civilized man, but may be developed by practice. Animals have this extra sense highly developed, and it plays a very important part in their protection from enemies; their capture of prey, etc. The strange actions of dogs, horses, etc., explained. How the geese saved Rome by reason of this sense. All hunters have experienced evidences of the existence of this sense on the part of animals. The physical telepathic sense. How it operates. Interesting instances of its possession by animals, and savage tribes. Women possess it strongly. The distinction between this form of thought-transference and clairvoyance.

LESSON - III

What "telepathy" means. The mental process by which one "knows at a distance." The sending and receiving of waves and currents of thought and feeling. Thought vibrations, and how they are caused. The part played by the cerebrum, cerebellum, and medulla oblongata—the three brains of man. The part played by the solar plexus and other great nervous centres. How thought messages are received. How states of emotional excitement are transmitted to others. The Pineal Gland: what it is, and

LESSON - VII

The second great method of securing clairvoyant en rapport relations with the astral plane. How the crystal, magic-mirror, etc., serves to focus the psychic energy of the clairvoyant person. The crystal serves the purpose of a psychic microscope or telescope. How crystals tend to become polarized to the vibrations of their owner. Why crystals should be preserved for the personal use of their owners. The use of crystals, or other forms of shining objects, by different peoples in ancient and modern times. How they are employed in Australia, New Zealand, Fiji Islands, South America, etc., by the primitive tribes. Various substitutes for the crystal. Full directions for Crystal Gazing. Complete instructions and warnings. All stages described, from the first "milky mist" to the clearly defined "psychic photograph." The Astral Tube, and the part it plays in Crystal Gazing. A complete little text-book of the subject.

LESSON VIII

The higher forms of Clairvoyance, and how they may be cultivated and acquired. Trance conditions not essential to highest Clairvoyance, although often connected therewith. In Clairvoyant Reverie, the clairvoyant does not become unconscious; but merely "shuts out" the outside world of sights and sounds. Shifting the consciousness from the physical plane to the astral. Clairvoyant Reverie may be safely and effectively induced by mental concentration alone. Artificial methods dangerous, and not advised by best authorities. Abnormal conditions not desirable. The "one pointed" mind. The Clairvoyant "day dream" or "brown study." False "psychic development." Use of hypnotic drugs strongly condemned. Scientific psychological methods stated and taught. The laws of attention and concentration of the mind. How Clairvoyance develops by this method. The true occult instruction given fully.

LESSON - IX

What the Clairvoyant senses in Simple Clairvoyance. Perception of the Aura, and Auric Emanations of others; Psychic Vibrations; Astral Colors; Thought Currents, Waves and Vibrations, etc., are features of Simple Clairvoyance. The beautiful kaleidoscopic spectacle of the Auric changes. The Prana Aura, and its appearances. The Mental and Emotional Aura, and its many interesting phases. Perception of Astral Thought-Forms. Other Astral Phenomena. The Astral World, and its Myriad Manifestations. Strange aspects of Astral Visioning. "Seeing through a Brick-wall." The X-Ray Vision. Reading from closed books, sealed envelopes, etc., and how it is explainable. Seeing into the depths of the earth, and the occult explanation thereof. The Laws and Principles of this Extraordinary Power. Magnifying and Diminishing Clairvoyant Vision. A wonderful field for experiment opened out for the student.

LESSON - X

The characteristics of Space Clairvoyance. The Astral Seeing of Distant Scenes; and through intervening objects. Remarkable instances of this power, well authenticated

How Cazotte foretold the coming of the French Revolution, including the fate of eminent personages present at the time of the prophecy. A startling occurrence, well worthy of careful study. The historical case of the assassination of Spencer Perceval, Chancellor of the Exchequer. Other well-authenticated cases. Symbolic visions. Irish and Scotch cases.

LESSON - XIV

Astral visioning in Clairvoyance, and visioning by means of the Astral Body. The difference between the two phases of clairvoyant phenomena. The characteristics of Astral-Body traveling. How one traveling in the Astral Body may "see all around him," instead of merely gazing at an astral picture. Limitations of Astral-Body visioning. What the Astral-Body really is; and what it is like. How it disengages itself from the physical body, and travels in space. Many persons "travel in the astral" during ordinary sleep. Occult teachings regarding Astral-Body traveling. How dying persons often travel in the astral-body, before death. Many interesting cases cited, all well-authenticated by scientific investigation. Society for Psychical Research's records and reports on such cases. Dangers of uninstructed persons going out on the astral, except in dream state. "Fools rush in where angels fear to tread." A timely warning. A most important and interesting subject.

LESSON - XV

Additional phases of Astral Phenomena. Projection of Thought-Forms. Something between ordinary Clairvoyance and Astral-Body perception. What a Thought-Form is. How it is created. What it does. Where it goes. How a portion of one's consciousness is projected in a Thought-Form. Using a Thought-Form as at cut-post, or observation point. How things appear when viewed from a Thought-Form. A wonderful phase of occult phenomena. Advantages and disadvantages of this form of clairvoyant visioning. Hindu Psychic Magic, and how it is performed. Remarkable illusory effects produced by Hindu Magicians. All is explained when the principle of the creation and projection of Thought-Forms is understood. Why the Hindus excel in this phase of occultism. An interesting description of Hindu Magic feats. The power of concentrated "visualization." The phenomena of Levitation, or the moving of articles at a distance. The occult explanation of this phenomenon. Natural explanation for so-called "super-natural" occurrence.

LESSON - XVI

The laws and principles underlying the power of one mind to influence and affect another mind. More than ordinary telepathy. The inductive power of mental vibrations. Everything is in vibration. Mental vibrations are much higher in the scale than are physical vibrations. What "induction" is. How a mental state, or an emotional feeling, tends to induce a similar state in another mind. Many instances cited. The different degrees of vibratory influence, and what causes the difference. The contagious effect of a "strong feeling." Why a strong desire hag a dynamic effect in certain cases. The power of visualization in Psychic Influence. The Attractive Power of Thought. The effect of Mental Concentration. Focusing your Forces. Holding the mind to a state of "one-pointedness." Why the occultist controls his imagination. Suggestions as to

LESSON - XX

The Psychic Principles underlying the many forms of psychic or mental healing. Many theories—one set of principles. Psychic Healing as old as the race. The Basic Principles of Psychic Healing. The Physiological Principles involved. How the Astral Body is used in Psychic Healing. Human Magnetism, and what it really is. All about Prana. The Laying-on of Hands in Healing; and what is back of it. What happens in Magnetic Healing. The Secret of Absent Healing. Space no barrier in Psychic Healing. The Human Aura and Psychic Healing. The Secret of Suggestive Therapeutics. The effect of the "affirmations" of the healers. How the Healing Cults obtain good results. Self-Healing by Psychic Power. Absent Healing by Psychic Power. How to "treat" others by Absent Treatment. Valuable Instructions and Practical Methods of Psychic Healing. The whole subject condensed, and made plain, so that it may be applied by any person of average intelligence. No fanciful theories; only plain, practical facts for actual application.

INTRODUCTION

In preparing this series of lessons for students of Western lands, I have been compelled to proceed along lines exactly opposite to those which I would have chosen had these lessons been for students in India. This because of the diametrically opposite mental attitudes of the students of these two several lands.

The student in India expects the teacher to state positively the principles involved, and the methods whereby these principles may be manifested, together with frequent illustrations (generally in the nature of fables or parables), serving to link the new knowledge to some already known thing. The Hindu student never expects or demands anything in the nature of "proof" of the teachers statements of principle or method; in fact, he would regard it as an insult to the teacher to ask for the same. Consequently, he does not look for, or ask, specific instances or illustrations in the nature of scientific evidence or proof of the principles taught. He may ask for more information, but solely for the purpose of bringing out some point which he has not grasped; but he avoids as a pestilence any question seeming to indicate argument, doubt of what is being taught him, or of the nature of a demand for proof or evidence.

The Western student, on the other hand, is accustomed to maintaining the skeptical attitude of mind—the scientific attitude of doubt and demand for proof—and the teacher so understands it. Both are accustomed to illustrations bringing out the principles involved, but these illustrations must not be fanciful or figurative—they must be actual cases, well authenticated and vouched for as evidence. In short, the Western teacher is expected to actually "prove" to his students his principles and methods, before he may expect them to be accepted. This, of course, not from any real doubt or suspicion of the veracity or ability of the teacher, but merely because the Western mind expects to question, and be questioned, in this way in the process of teaching and learning. Consequently, in this series of lessons, I have sought to follow the Western method rather than the Hindu. So far as is possible, I have avoided the flat positive statement of principles and methods, and have sought to prove each step of the teaching. Of course, I have been compelled to assume the existence of certain fundamental principles, in order to avoid long and technical metaphysical and philosophical discussions. I have also had to content myself with the positive flat assertion of the existence of the Astral Plane, Akashic Records, Prana, etc., which are fundamental postulates of Hindu philosophy and occult science—for these are established solely by the experience of those who are able to function on the higher planes themselves. But, beyond this I have sought to prove by direct and positive evidence (adapted to the Western mind) every step of my teaching and methods.

In offering this scientific proof, I have purposely omitted (except in a few instances) all mention of occult or psychic phenomena occurring in India, and have confined myself to instances occurring in Western lands to Western persons. Moreover, I have avoided quoting and citing Hindu authorities, and have, instead, quoted and cited from authorities well known and respected in Western lands, such as the Society for Psychical Research, and the prominent scientists interested in the work of the said society. In this way I have sought to furnish the Western student with examples, cases, and illustrations familiar to him, and easily referred to. Had I cited Indian cases, I might be accused of offering proof that could not be easily verified; and quoting persons unknown to my readers. There is a wealth of such cases and illustration in India, naturally, but these as a rule are traditional and not available in printed form; and these would not likely be very satisfactory to the Western student.

I must, however, positively and firmly state that while these cases and illustrations, these quotations and citations, are purely Western, the principles they illustrate and prove are among the oldest known to Hindu occult science and philosophy. In fact, having been accepted as proved truth in India, for centuries past, there is very little demand for further proof thereof on the part of the Hindus. In the Western world, however, these things are comparatively new, and must be proved and attested accordingly. So, as I have said, I have cut the cloth of my instruction to conform with the pattern favored for the Western garment of knowledge. So far as the illustrations and cases, the quotations and citations are concerned—these are purely Western and familiar to the student. But, when it comes to the principles themselves, this is another matter—I must be pardoned for stating that these are the outgrowth of Hindu thought and investigation, and that he who would discover their roots must dig around the tree of the Wisdom of the East, which has stood the storms and winds of thousands of years. But the branches of this mighty tree are wide-spreading, and there is room for many Western students to rest in its shade and shelter.

In these lessons I have referred occasionally to my two little books, entitled "The Astral World," and "The Human Aura," respectively. To those who are interested in these subjects, I recommend these little books; they are sold at a nominal price, and contain much that will be helpful to the student of Hindu Occult Science. They are not required, however, to complete the understanding of the subjects treated upon in these lessons, and are mentioned and recommended merely as supplementary reading for the student who wishes to take little "side excursions" away from the main trip covered in these lessons.

I trust that my students will find the pleasure and satisfaction in studying these lessons that I have in writing them.

May, 1916 **SWAMI PANCHADASI**

LESSON - I

THE ASTRAL SENSES

The student of occultism usually is quite familiar with the crass individual who assumes the cheap skeptical attitude toward occult matters, which attitude he expresses in his would-be "smart" remark that he "believes only in what his senses perceive." He seems to think that his cheap wit has finally disposed of the matter, the implication being that the occultist is a credulous, "easy" person who believes in the existence of things contrary to the evidence of the senses.

While the opinion or views of persons of this class are, of course, beneath the serious concern of any true student of occultism, nevertheless the mental attitude of such persons are worthy of our passing consideration, inasmuch as it serves to give us an object lesson regarding the childlike attitude of the average so-called "practical" persons regarding the matter of the evidence of the senses.

These so-called practical persons have much to say regarding their senses. They are fond of speaking of "the evidence of my senses." They also have much to say about the possession of "good sense" on their part; of having "sound common sense"; and often they make the strange boast that they have "horse sense," seeming to consider this a great possession. Alas, for the pretensions of this class of persons. They are usually found quite credulous regarding matters beyond their everyday field of work and thought, and accept without question the most ridiculous teachings and dogmas reaching them from the voice of some claimed authority, while they sneer at some advanced teaching which their minds are incapable of comprehending. Anything which seems unusual to them is deemed "flighty," and lacking in appeal to their much prized "horse sense."

But, it is not my intention to spend time in discussing these insignificant half-penny intellects. I have merely alluded to them in order to bring to your mind the fact that to many persons the idea of "sense" and that of "senses" is very closely allied. They consider all knowledge and wisdom as "sense;" and all such sense as being derived directly from their ordinary five senses.

They ignore almost completely the intuitional phases of the mind, and are unaware of many of the higher processes of reasoning.

Such persons accept as undoubted anything that their senses report to them. They consider it heresy to question a report of the senses. One of their favorite remarks is that "it almost makes me doubt my senses." They fail to perceive that their senses, at the best, are very imperfect instruments, and that the mind is constantly employed in correcting the mistaken report of the ordinary five senses.

Not to speak of the common phenomenon of color-blindness, in which one color seems to be another, our senses are far from being exact. We may, by suggestion, be made to imagine that we smell or taste certain things which do not exist, and hypnotic subjects may be caused to see things that have no existence save in the imagination of the person. The familiar experiment of the person crossing his first two fingers, and placing them on a small object, such as a pea or the top of a lead-pencil, shows us how "mixed" the sense of feeling becomes at times. The many familiar instances of optical delusions show us that even our sharp eyes may deceive us—every conjuror knows how easy it is to deceive the eye by suggestion and false movements.

Perhaps the most familiar example of mistaken sense-reports is that of the movement of the earth. The senses of every person report to him that the earth is a fixed, immovable body, and that the sun, moon, planets, and stars move around the earth every twenty-four hours. It is only when one accepts the reports of the reasoning faculties, that he knows that the earth not only whirls around on its axis every twenty-four hours, but that it circles around the sun every three hundred and sixty-five days; and that even the sun itself, carrying with it the earth and the other planets, really moves along in space, moving toward or around some unknown point far distant from it. If there is any one particular report of the senses which would seem to be beyond doubt or question, it certainly would be this elementary sense report of the fixedness of the earth beneath our feet, and the movements of the heavenly bodies around it—and yet we know that this is merely an illusion, and that the facts of the case are totally different. Again, how few persons really realize that the eye perceives things up-side-down, and that the mind only gradually acquires the trick of adjusting the impression?

I am not trying to make any of you doubt the report of his or her five senses. That would be most foolish, for all of us must needs depend upon these five senses in our everyday affairs, and would soon come to grief were we to neglect their reports. Instead, I am trying to acquaint you with the real nature of these five senses, that you may realize what they are not, as well as what they are; and also that you may realize that there is no absurdity in believing that there are more channels of information open to the ego, or soul of the person, than these much used five senses. When you once get a correct scientific conception of the real nature of the five ordinary senses, you will be able to intelligently grasp the nature of the higher psychic faculties or senses, and thus be better fitted to use them. So, let us take a few moments time in order to get this fundamental knowledge well fixed in our minds.

What are the five senses, anyway. Your first answer will be: "Feeling, seeing, hearing, tasting, smelling." But that is merely a recital of the different forms of sensing. What is a "sense," when you get right down to it? Well, you will find that the dictionary tells us that a sense is a "faculty, possessed by animals, of perceiving external objects by means of impressions made upon certain organs of the body." Getting right down to the roots of the matter, we find that the five senses of man are the channels through which he becomes aware or conscious of information concerning objects outside of himself. But, these senses are not the sense-organs alone. Back of the organs there is a peculiar arrangement of the nervous system, or brain centres, which take up the messages received through the organs; and back of this, again, is the ego, or soul, or mind, which, at the last, is the real KNOWER. The eye is merely a camera; the ear, merely a receiver of sound-waves; the nose, merely an arrangement of sensitive mucous membrane; the mouth and tongue, simply a container of taste-buds; the nervous system, merely a sensitive apparatus designed to transmit messages to the brain and other centres—all being but part of the physical machinery, and liable to impairment or destruction. Back of all this apparatus is the real Knower who makes use of it.

Science tells us that of all the five senses, that of Touch or Feeling was the original—the fundamental sense. All the rest are held to be but modifications of, and specialized forms of, this original sense of feeling. I am telling you this not merely in the way of interesting and instructive scientific information, but also because an understanding of this fact will enable you to more clearly comprehend that which I shall have to say to you about the higher faculties or senses.

Many of the very lowly and simple forms of animal life have this one sense only, and that but poorly developed. The elementary life form "feels" the touch of its food, or of other objects which may touch it. The plants also have something akin to this sense, which in some cases, like that of the Sensitive Plant, for instance, is quite well developed. Long before the sense of sight, or the sensitiveness to light appeared in animal-life, we find evidences of taste, and something like rudimentary hearing or sensitiveness to sounds. Smell gradually developed from the sense of taste, with which even now it is closely connected. In some forms of lower animal life the sense of smell is much more highly developed than in mankind. Hearing evolved in due time from the rudimentary feeling of vibrations. Sight, the highest of the senses, came last, and was an evolution of the elementary sensitiveness to light.

But, you see, all these senses are but modifications of the original sense of feeling or touch. The eye records the touch or feeling of the light-waves which strike upon it. The ear records the touch or feeling of the sound-waves or vibrations of the air, which reach it. The tongue and other seats of taste record the chemical touch of the particles of food, or other substances, coming in contact with the taste-buds. The nose records the chemical touch of the gases or fine particles of material which touch its mucous membrane. The sensory-nerves record the presence of outer objects coming in contact with the nerve ends in various parts of the skin of the body. You see that all of these senses merely record the contact or "touch" of outside objects.

But the sense organs, themselves, do not do the knowing of the presence of the objects. They are but pieces of delicate apparatus serving to record or to receive primary impressions from outside. Wonderful as they are, they have their counterparts in the works of man, as for instance: the camera, or artificial eye; the phonograph, or, artificial ear; the delicate chemical apparatus, or artificial taster and smeller; the telegraph, or artificial nerves. Not only this, but there are always to be found nerve telegraph wires conveying the messages of the eye, the ear, the nose, the tongue, to the brain—telling the something in the brain of what has been felt at the other end of the line. Sever the nerves leading to the eye, and though the eye will continue to register perfectly, still no message will reach the brain. And render the brain unconscious, and no message will reach it from the nerves connecting with eye, ear, nose, tongue, or surface of the body. There is much more to the receiving of sense messages than you would think at first, you see.

Now all this means that the ego, or soul, or mind, if you prefer the term—is the real Knower who becomes aware of the outside world by means of the messages of the senses. Cut off from these messages the mind would be almost a blank, so far as outside objects are concerned. Every one of the senses so cut off would mean a diminishing or cutting-off of a part of the world of the ego. And, likewise, each new sense added to the list tends to widen and increase the world of the ego. We do not realize this, as a rule. Instead, we are in the habit of thinking that the world consists of just so many things and facts, and that we know every possible one of them. This is the reasoning of a child. Think how very much smaller than the world of the average person is the world of the person born blind, or the person born deaf! Likewise, think how very much greater and wider, and more wonderful this world of ours would seem were each of us to find ourselves suddenly endowed with a new sense! How much more we would perceive. How much more we would feel. How much more we would know. How much more we would have to talk about. Why, we are really in about the same position as the poor girl, born blind, who said that she thought that the color of scarlet must be something like the sound of a trumpet. Poor thing, she could form no conception of color, never having seen a ray of light—she could think and speak only in the terms of touch, sound, taste and smell. Had she also been deaf, she would have been robbed of a still greater share of her world. Think over these things a little.

Suppose, on the contrary, that we had a new sense which would enable us to sense the waves of electricity. In that case we would be able to "feel" what was going on at another place—perhaps on the other side of the world, or maybe, on one of the other planets. Or, suppose that we had an X Ray sense—we could then see through a stone wall, inside the rooms of a house. If our vision were improved by the addition of a telescopic adjustment, we could see what is going on in Mars, and could send and receive communications with those living there. Or, if with a microscopic adjustment, we could see all the secrets of a drop of water—maybe it is well that we cannot do this. On the other hand, if we had a well-developed telepathic sense, we would be aware of the thought-waves of others to such an extent that there would be no secrets left hidden to anyone—wouldn't that alter life and human intercourse a great deal? These things would really be no more wonderful than is the evolution of the senses we have. We can do some of these things by apparatus designed by the brain of man—and man really is but an imitator and adaptor of Nature. Perhaps, on some other world or planet there may be beings having seven, nine or fifteen senses, instead of the poor little five known to us. Who knows!

But it is not necessary to exercise the imagination in the direction of picturing beings on other planets endowed with more senses than have the people of earth. While, as the occult teachings positively state, there are beings on other planets whose senses are as much higher than the earth-man's as the latter's are higher than those of the oyster, still we do not have to go so far to find instances of the possession of much higher and more active faculties than those employed by the ordinary man. We have but to consider the higher psychical faculties of man, right here and now, in order to see what new worlds are open to him. When you reach a scientific understanding of these things, you will see that there really is nothing at all supernatural about much of the great body of wonderful experiences of men in all times which the "horse sense" man sneeringly dismisses as "queer" and "contrary to sense." You will see that these experiences are quite as natural as are those in which the ordinary five senses are employed—though they are super-physical. There is the greatest difference between supernatural and super-physical, you must realize.

All occultists know that man has other senses than the ordinary five, although but few men have developed them sufficiently well to use them effectively. These super-physical senses are known to the occultists as "the astral senses." The term "Astral," used so frequently by all occultists, ancient and modern, is derived from the Greek word "astra," meaning "star." It is used to indicate those planes of being immediately above the physical plane. The astral senses are really the counterparts of the physical senses of man, and are connected with the astral body of the person just as the physical senses are connected with the physical body. The office of these astral senses is to enable the person to receive impressions on the astral plane, just as his physical senses enable him to receive impressions on the physical plane. On the physical plane the mind of man receives only the sense impressions of the physical organs of sense; but when the mind functions and vibrates on the astral plane, it requires astral senses in order to receive the impressions of that plane, and these, as we shall see, are present.

Each one of the physical senses of man has its astral counterpart. Thus man has, in latency, the power of seeing, feeling, tasting, smelling, and hearing, on the astral plane, by means of his five astral senses. More than this, the best occultists know that man really has seven physical senses instead of but five, though these two additional senses are not unfolded in the case of the average person (though occultists who have reached a certain stage are able to use them effectively). Even these two extra physical senses have their counterparts on the astral plane.

Persons who have developed the use of their astral senses are able to receive the sense impressions of the astral plane just as clearly as they receive those of the physical plane by means of the physical senses. For instance, the person is thus able to perceive things occurring on the astral plane; to read the Akashic Records of the past; to perceive things that are happening in other parts of the world; to see past happenings as well; and in cases of peculiar development, to catch glimpses of the future, though this is far rarer than the other forms of astral sight.

Again, by means of clairaudience, the person may hear the things of the astral world, past as well as present, and in rare cases, the future. The explanation is the same in each case—merely the receiving of vibrations on the astral plane instead of on the physical plane. In the same way, the astral senses of smelling, tasting, and feeling operate. But though we have occasional instances of astral feeling, in certain phases of psychic phenomena, we have practically no manifestation of astral smelling or tasting, although the astral senses are there ready for use. It is only in instances of travelling in the astral body that the last two mentioned astral senses, viz., smell and taste, are manifested.

The phenomena of telepathy, or thought transference, occurs on both the physical and the mental plane. On the physical plane it is more or less spontaneous and erratic in manifestation; while on the astral plane it is as clear, reliable and responsive to demand as is astral sight, etc.

The ordinary person has but occasional flashes of astral sensing, and as a rule is not able to experience the phenomenon at will. The trained occultist, on the contrary, is able to shift from one set of senses to the other, by a simple act or effort of will, whenever he may wish to do so. Advanced occultists are often able to function on both physical and astral planes at the same time, though they do not often desire to do so. To vision astrally, the trained occultist merely shifts his sensory mechanism from physical to astral, or vice versa, just as the typewriter operator shifts from the small-letter type to the capitals, by simply touching the shift-key of his machine.

Many persons suppose that it is necessary to travel on the astral plane, in the astral body, in order to use the astral senses. This is a mistake. In instances of clairvoyance, astral visioning, psychometry, etc., the occultist remains in his physical body, and senses the phenomena of the astral plane quite readily, by means of the astral senses, just as he is able to sense the phenomena of the physical plane when he uses the physical organs—quite more easily, in fact, in many instances. It is not even necessary for the occultist to enter into the trance condition, in the majority of cases.

Travel in the astral body is quite another phase of occult phenomena, and is far more difficult to manifest. The student should never attempt to travel in the astral body except under the instruction of some competent instructor.

In Crystal Gazing, the occultist merely employs the crystal in order to concentrate his power, and to bring to a focus his astral vision. There is no supernatural virtue in the crystal itself—it is merely a means to an end; a piece of useful apparatus to aid in the production of certain phenomena.

In Psychometry some object is used in order to bring the occulist "en rapport" with the person or thing associated with it. But it is the astral senses which are employed in describing either the past environment of the thing, or else the present or past doings of the person in question, etc. In short, the object is merely the loose end of the psychic ball of twine which the psychometrist proceeds to wind or unwind at will. Psychometry is merely one form of astral seeing; just as is crystal gazing.

In what is known as Telekinesis, or movement at a distance, there is found the employment of both astral sensing, and astral will action accompanied in many cases by actual projection of a portion of the substance of the astral body.

In the case of Clairvoyance, we have an instance of the simplest form of astral seeing, without the necessity of the "associated object" of psychometry, or the focal point of the crystal in crystal gazing.

This is true not only of the ordinary form of clairvoyance, in which the occultist sees astrally the happenings and doings at some distant point, at the moment of observation; it is also true of what is known as past clairvoyance, or astral seeing of past events; and in the seeing of future events, as in prophetic vision, etc. These are all simply different forms of one and the same thing.

Surely, some of you may say, "These things are supernatural, far above the realm of natural law—and yet this man would have us believe otherwise."

Softly, softly, dear reader, do not jump at conclusions so readily. What do you know about the limits of natural law and phenomena? What right have you to assert that all beyond your customary range of sense experience is outside of Nature? Do you not realize that you are attempting to place a limit upon Nature, which in reality is illimitable?

The man of a generation back of the present one would have been equally justified in asserting that the marvels of wireless telegraphy were supernatural, had he been told of the possibility of their manifestation. Going back a little further, the father of that man would have said the same thing regarding the telephone, had anyone been so bold as to have prophesied it. Going back still another generation, imagine the opinion of some of the old men of that time regarding the telegraph. And yet these things are simply the discovery and application of certain of Nature's wonderful powers and forces.

Is it any more unreasonable to suppose that Nature has still a mine of undiscovered treasure in the mind and constitution of man, as well as in inorganic nature? No, friends, these things are as natural as the physical senses, and not a whit more of a miracle. It is only that we are accustomed to one, and not to the other, that makes the astral senses seem more wonderful than the physical. Nature's workings are all wonderful—none more so than the other. All are beyond our absolute conception, when we get down to their real essence. So let us keep an open mind!

LESSON - II

TELEPATHY vs. CLAIRVOYANCE

In this work I shall use the term "clairvoyance" in its broad sense of "astral perception," as distinguished from perception by means of the physical senses. As we proceed, you will see the general and special meanings of the term, so there is no necessity for a special definition or illustration of the term at this time.

By "telepathy," I mean the sending and receiving of thought messages, and mental and emotional states, consciously or unconsciously, by means of what may be called "the sixth sense" of the physical plane. There is, of course, a form of thought transference on the astral plane, but this I include under the general term of clairvoyance, for reasons which will be explained later on.

You will remember that in the preceding chapter I told you that in addition to the five ordinary physical senses of man there were also two other physical senses comparatively undeveloped in the average person. These two extra physical senses are, respectively, (1) the sense of the presence of other living things; and (2) the telepathic sense. As I also told you, these two extra physical senses have their astral counterparts. They also have certain physical organs which are not generally recognized by physiologists or psychologists, but which are well known to all occultists. I shall now consider the first of the two above-mentioned extra physical senses, in order to clear the way for our consideration of the question of the distinction between ordinary telepathy and that form of clairvoyance which is its astral counterpart.

There is in every human being a sense which is not generally recognized as such, although nearly every person has had more or less experience regarding its workings. I refer to the sense of the presence of other living things, separate and apart from the operation of any of the five ordinary physical senses. I ask you to understand that I am not claiming that this is a higher sense than the other physical senses, or that it has come to man in a high state of evolution. On the contrary, this sense came to living things far back in the scale of evolution. It is possessed by the higher forms of the lower animals, such as the horse, dog, and the majority of the wild beasts. Savage and barbaric men have it more highly developed than it is in the case of the civilized man. In fact, this physical sense may be termed almost vestigal in civilized man, because he has not actively used it for many generations. For that matter, the physical sense of smell is also deficient in man, and for the same reason, whereas in the case of the lower animals, and savage man, the sense of smell is very keen. I mention this for fear of misunderstanding. In my little book, "The Astral World," I have said: "All occultists know that man really has seven senses, instead of merely five, though the additional two senses are not sufficiently developed for use in the average person (though the occultist generally unfolds them into use)." Some have taken this to mean that the occultist develops these two extra physical senses, just as he does certain higher psychic or astral faculties. But this is wrong. The occultist, in such case, merely re-awakens these two senses which have been almost lost to the race. By use and exercise he then develops them to a wonderful proficiency, for use on the physical plane.

Now, this sense of the presence of other living beings is very well developed in the lower animals, particularly in those whose safety depends upon the knowledge of the presence of their natural enemies. As might be expected, the wild animals have it more highly developed than do the domesticated animals. But even among the latter, we find instances of this sense being in active use—in the case of dogs, horses, geese, etc., especially. Who of us is not familiar with the strange actions of the dog, or the horse, when the animal senses the unseen and unheard presence of some person or animal? Very often we would scold or punish the animal for its peculiar actions, simply because we are not able to see what is worrying it. How often does the dog start suddenly, and bristle up its hair, when nothing is in sight, or within hearing distance. How often does the horse grow "skittish," or even panicky, when there is nothing within sight or hearing. Domestic fowls, especially geese, manifest an uneasiness at the presence of strange persons or animals, though they may not be able to see or hear them. It is a matter of history that this sense, in a flock of geese, once saved ancient Rome from an attack of the enemy. The night was dark and stormy, and the trained eyesight and keen hearing of the Roman outposts failed to reveal the approach of the enemy. But, the keen sense of the geese felt the presence of strange men, and they started to cackle loudly, aroused the guard, and Rome was saved. Skeptical persons have sought to explain this historical case by the theory that the geese heard the approaching enemy. But this explanation will not serve, for the Roman soldiers were marching about on their posts and guard-duty, and the geese remained silent until they sensed the approach of the small number of the enemy's scouts, when they burst into wild cries. The ancient Romans, themselves, were under no illusion about the matter—they recognized the existence of some unusual power in the geese, and they gave the animals the full credit therefor.

Hunters in wild and strange lands have told us that often when they were lying concealed for the purpose of shooting the wild animals when they came within range, they have witnessed instances of the existence of this strange faculty in the wild beasts. Though they could not see the concealed hunters, nor smell them (as the wind was in the other direction) all of a sudden one or more of the animals (generally an old female) would start suddenly, and a shiver would be seen to pass over its body; then it would utter a low warning note, and away would fly the pack. Nearly every hunter has had the experience of watching his expected game, when all of a sudden it would start off with a nervous jerk, and without waiting to sniff the air, as is usual, would bolt precipitately from the scene. Moreover, many beasts of prey are known to sense the presence of their natural prey, even when the wind is in the other direction, and there is no sound or movement made by the crouching, fearstricken animal. Certain birds seem to sense the presence of particular worms upon which they feed, though the latter be buried several inches in the earth, or in the bark of trees.

Savage man also has this faculty developed, as all travellers and explorers well know. They are as keen as a wild animal to sense the nearness of enemies, or, in some cases, the approach of man-eating beasts. This does not mean that that these savages are more highly developed than is civilized man—quite the reverse. This is the explanation: when man became more civilized, and made himself more secure from his wild-beast enemies, as well as from the sudden attacks of his human enemies, he began to use this sense less and less. Finally, in the course of many generations, it became almost atrophied from disuse, and ceased reporting to the brain, or other nerve centres. Or, if you prefer viewing it from another angle, it may be said that the nerve centres, and brain, began to pay less and less attention to the reports of this sense (trusting more to sight and hearing) until the consciousness failed to awaken to the reports. You know how your consciousness will finally refuse to be awakened by familiar sounds (such as the noise of machinery in the shop, or ordinary noises in the house), although the ears receive the sound-waves.

Well, this is the way in the case of this neglected sense—for the two reasons just mentioned, the average person is almost unaware of its existence. Almost unaware I have said—not totally unaware. For probably every one of us has had experiences in which we have actually "felt" the presence of some strange person about the premises, or place. The effect of the report of this sense is particularly noticed in the region of the solar plexus, or the pit of the stomach. It manifests in a peculiar, unpleasant feeling of "gone-ness" in that region—it produces a feeling of "something wrong," which disturbs one in a strange way. This is generally accompanied by a "bristling up," or "creepy" feeling along the spine. The organs registering the presence of a strange or alien creature consist of certain delicate nerves of the surface of the skin, generally connected with the roots of the downy hair of the body—or resting where the hair roots would naturally be, in the case of a hairless skin. These seem to report directly to the solar-plexus, which then acts quickly by reflex action on the other parts of the body, causing an instinctive feeling to either fly the scene or else to crouch and hide oneself. This feeling, as may be seen at once, is an inheritance from our savage ancestors, or perhaps from our lowly-animal ancestral roots. It is a most unpleasant feeling, and the race escapes much discomfort by reason of its comparative absence.

I have said that occultists have developed, or rather re-developed this sense. They do this in order to have a harmonious well-developed seven-fold sense system. It increases their general "awareness." Certain other knowledge of the occultist neutralizes the unpleasant features of the manifestation of this sense, and he finds it often a very valuable adjunct to his senses of seeing and hearing, particularly in the cases in which he is approached by persons having antagonistic or hostile feelings toward him, as in such cases this faculty is particularly active. In connection with the telepathic sense (to be described a little further on) this sense operates to give a person that sense of warning when approached by another person whose feelings are not friendly to him, no matter how friendly the outward appearance of that person may be. These two extra senses co-operate to give a person that instinctive feeling of warning, which all of us know in our own experience.

This particular, as well as the telepathic sense, may be cultivated or developed by anyone who wishes to take the time and trouble to accomplish the work. The principle is simple—merely the same principle that one uses in developing any of the other physical attributes, namely, use and exercise. The first step (a) is the recognition of the existence of the sense itself; then (b) the attention given to its reports; then (c) frequent use and exercise. Just think of how you would proceed to develop any of the five ordinary senses—the hearing, sight, or touch, for instance—then follow the same process in the cultivation of this extra sense, or two senses, and you will accomplish the same kind of results.

Now, let us consider the other extra physical sense—the "telepathic" sense, or sense of becoming aware of the thought-waves, or emotional waves, of other persons. Now, as strange as this may appear to some persons—the most of persons in fact—this telepathic faculty is not a "higher" faculty or sense, but is really a comparatively low one. Just like the sense just described, it is possessed in a higher degree by many of the lower animals, and by primitive and savage man. That which really is "higher" in this kind of psychic phenomena is the manifestation of that higher form of telepathy—by use of the astral counterpart of this sense—which we shall consider, later, under the name of clairvoyance, for this is really a particular phase of clairvoyance.

As strange as it may appear to some of you, the lower animals possess a kind of telepathic sense. An animal is usually aware of your feelings toward it, and your purposes regarding it. Domestic animals lose some of this by generations of confinement, while the wild animals have the sense highly developed. But even some of the domestic animals have more or less of it. You will readily recognize this fact if you have ever tried to "cut out" a certain animal from a herd or flock. You will find that the animal in some way has sensed your designs upon it, no matter how indirectly you approach it, and it will begin circling around the other animals, twisting in and out in its endeavors to be lost to your sight. The other animals, likewise, will seem to know that you are after only that particular one, and will manifest but little fright or distrust, comparatively.

I have frequently seen this thing, in my own country and in others, among poultry raisers. The poultryman will think, to himself, "Now, I am going to get that black hen with the yellow legs—that fat, clumsy one," and he will move toward the flock slowly and with an air of unconcern. But, lo! as soon as he gets near the creatures, that black hen will be seen edging her way to the outer circle of the flock, on the opposite side from the man. When the man moves around to her side, she will be found to have plunged into the crowd, and it is hard to find her. Sometimes she will actually try to sneak off, and conceal herself in some dark corner, or back of some large object. Every poultryman will smile when this occurrence is mentioned to him—he knows by experience that hens have a way of sensing what he has in his mind regarding them.

Moreover, as every farmer knows, the crow family has a most uncanny way of sensing the intentions of the farmer who is trying to destroy them, and shows great sagacity in defeating those intentions. But, while the crow is a very intelligent bird—one of the wisest of the bird family, in fact—it obtains its knowledge of what is in the mind of the man not alone from "figuring on his intentions," but rather from that instinctive sensing of his mental states. The hen, as all know, is a very stupid bird, showing but little intelligent activity. But, nevertheless, she is very quick about sensing the poultryman's designs on her, though generally very stupid about planning out a skillful escape.

Every owner of dogs, cats and horses, has had many opportunities for observing the manifestation of this sense on the part of those animals. Every dog feels the emotional states of his owner, and others. The horse knows when his owner seeks to throw the halter over his neck, or when, on the contrary, he is merely walking through the field. Cats sense their owners' feelings and thoughts, and often resent them. Of course, the lower animals can sense merely elementary mental states, and generally *only* emotional states, as their minds are not developed so as to interpret the more complex mental states. Primitive men likewise almost instinctively sense the feelings and designs of other men. They do not reason the thing out, but rather merely "feel" the ideas and designs of the others. The women of the lower races are more adept in interpreting these sense reports than are the men. Women are more sensitive, as a rule, than are men—on any point on the scale of development.

When we come to consider ordinary telepathy in the case of men of civilized countries, we find a more complex state of affairs. While civilized man, as a whole, has lost some of the quick telepathic perception of the lower races, he has, in some exceptional cases, acquired a faculty of receiving and interpreting more complex thought-forms and mental states. The investigations of the Society for Psychical Research, and those of private investigators as well, have shown us that a picture of a complicated geometrical design held in the mind of one person may be carried to and received by the mind of another person, who reproduces the design on paper. In the same way, complicated thoughts have been transmitted and received. But these are only exceptional cases. In many cases this sense seems almost dead in the ordinary civilized individual, except when aroused in exceptional cases.

But, nevertheless, the majority of persons have occasional flashes of telepathy—just enough to make them realize that "there is something in it." The renewed interest in the subject, of late years, has directed the public mind to the phenomena of telepathy, and, consequently, more persons are now taking note of the cases of thought-transference coming under their personal notice. It must be remembered, of course, that all of us are constantly receiving thought-waves, and feeling thought-influence, unconsciously. I am speaking now only of the conscious perception of the thought-waves.

Many investigators have so developed their telepathic sense that they are able, at times, to obtain wonderful test results. But, it has been a source of disappointment to many of them to discover that at other times, under apparently similar conditions, their success was very slight. So true is this that many authorities have accepted the theory that telepathy is more or less spontaneous, and cannot be produced to order. This theory is true as far as it goes, but there is a side of the case that these investigators overlook, probably because of their lack of the occult principles involved in the phenomena. I mean this: that their most brilliant successes have been obtained by reason of their unconscious "switching on" of the astral telepathic sense, the clairvoyant sense. While in this condition, they obtained startling results; but the next time they tried, they failed to awaken the astral sense, and, therefore, had to depend entirely upon the physical telepathic sense, and, consequently, their results were comparatively poor.

You will understand the difference and distinction between physical-sense telepathy, and astral-sense telepathy, if you will carefully consider the nature of each, as I shall now present it to you. I ask your close attention to what I shall have to say on this subject in the remaining pages of this chapter. Do not pass over these explanations as "dry," for unless you have a clear fundamental understanding of the thing, you will never be able to get the best results. This is true of every phase of learning, physical as well as psychical—one must get started right, in order to obtain the best results.

In the first place, every thought process, every emotional activity, every creation of ideas, is accompanied by a manifestation of force—in fact, is the result of the manifestation of a force. Without entering at all into the question of what mind is, in itself, we may rest firmly on the natural fact that every manifestation of mental or emotional activity is the result of an action of the brain or nervous system, manifesting in a form of vibrations. Just as in the case of the manifestation of electricity in which certain chemical elements are consumed, or transformed, so in the case of mental or emotional activity there is a consuming or transformation of the substance of which the nervous system is composed. When I say "nervous system" in this connection, I include the brain, or brains of man—for these are but a part of his great nervous system in which all emotional or mental activity is manifested.

Moreover, just as there is no real destruction of matter in any of Nature's processes—all seeming destruction being but a transformation—so in the case before us there is a transformation of the energy released in the thought or emotional process. We may grasp this idea more clearly if we consider what takes place into transformation of electrical energy. For instance, transmit a strong current of electricity over a fine wire, or filament of carbon, and lo! the current is transformed into light. Use another kind of channel of transmission, and the current is transformed into heat. Every electric light, or electric heating apparatus is proof of this. In the same way, the electric current is sent into space in the form of wireless waves. These waves coming in contact with certain forms of apparatus are transformed into forms of force which are registered and interpreted by the wireless operator.

In the same way, the telepathic waves of energy are sent forth by the activity released by the thought or emotion state. These waves travel in every direction, and when they come in contact with physical apparatus sufficiently sensitive to register them, they may be reproduced or retransformed into thought or mental states similar to those which originally sent them forth. You talk into the receiver of the telephone, and the sound waves are transformed into waves of electricity. These electric waves travel over the wires, and on reaching the other end of the telephone circuit are again transformed into sound-waves which are heard by the ear of the listener. Well, then, when your brain sends out thought waves, these travel until they are received by the apparatus in the brain of another person, when they are re-transformed into thoughts of the same kind that originally caused the thought-waves. I will have much more to say on this subject in the next chapter. I will pause here to point out the difference between the phenomena of this form of telepathy, and the higher form which is really a phase of clairvoyance.

Now, in the case of what may be called a clairvoyant-telepathy, or astral telepathy, the ordinary thought-waves play but a small part. Instead of these, there is a transmission of force along the channels of the astral plane. It is almost impossible to describe the phenomena of the astral plane in the terms of the physical. I may illustrate the matter, in a general way, by saying that is something like your astral self actually extending itself out until it touches the astral self of the other person, and thus actually "feels" the astral activities there, instead of it being a case of something like waves travelling along space between brain and brain. Do you get this clearly? This is about as near to it as I can explain it to you at this place. Telepathy is simply a matter of the transmission and receiving of waves of vibratory force which have travelled along the ether between two persons. But clairvoyance or astral-telepathy is something like your mind being extended out until it actually touches the mind of the other person and sees what is there.

I shall have much to say regarding the working out of the processes of clairvoyance, as we proceed. I have merely given the above explanation for the purpose of distinguishing between ordinary telepathy and clairvoyance, so as to prevent you from falling into a common error. Now let us consider the phenomena of ordinary telepathy—this is very wonderful in itself, although it is on a lower plane of activity than its astral or clairvoyant counterpart.

LESSON - III

TELEPATHY EXPLAINED

Telepathy, meaning Thought-Transference, bears a misleading title. Literally translated, it means "suffering at a distance," or, perhaps, "feeling pain at a distance." The name should really indicate "knowing at a distance," in order to be properly descriptive. But as the term has acquired a forced meaning by reason of years of usage, it will probably be continued in popular favor. After all, names do not count, so long as the meaning is accepted and understood.

While the term itself has been generally used in the sense of conscious and deliberate sending and receiving of thought-waves, there is a far wider field of phenomena really covered by it, viz., the unconscious sending and receiving of mental and emotional vibrations. I shall take up this phase of the subject in a moment, after I have called your attention to the mechanism whereby the waves of thought and emotion are transmitted.

In the last chapter, you will remember that I called your attention to the fact that there is a manifestation of energy or force (in the form of vibrations) in every mental or emotional state. This is true not only in the case of deep thought or vivid feeling, but also in the case of general mental "feelings," and emotional states. During such manifestations there is a radiation of mental or emotional vibrations from the brain or nervous centres of the system, which flows out in all directions just as do light and wireless electricity. The principal seats or centres of these radiations are (1) the several brains of man, viz., the cerebrum, cerebellum, and the medulla oblongata, respectfully; and (2) the several great centres of nerve substance in the human system, called the plexi, such as the solar plexus, etc.

The vibrations arising from emotional excitement are sent out principally from the plexi, or great centres of the sympathetic nervous system. Those arising from the more strictly mental states emanate from certain centres and points of the brain, or brains, of the person manifesting them. Certain forms of these vibrations constitute the real essence of what is generally called "human magnetism," which will be treated upon in the proper place in these lessons.

I do not think it advisable to go into the technical details of the generation and mechanism of transmission of these thought and emotional vibrations, in these lessons. To understand the same would require a technical knowledge of physiology and organic chemistry, which is not possessed by the average person. Moreover, such details are neither interesting nor instructive to the general student of occultism. But, I think it proper to give at least a brief description of the receiving of such vibratory-waves by other individuals.

In the first place, every great plexus, or groups of nerve ganglia, in the human system is a receiving station, as well as a sending station. A person manifesting strong emotional excitement tends to awaken similar states in the nervous centres of other persons in whom the conditions are favorable. This explains why the vibrations of anger, fear, panic, are so contagious. It also explains the strong effect of the vibrations emanating from the nerve centres controlling the reproductive system, in certain cases of strong sexual excitation. Each human sympathetic nervous system contains many receiving stations where emotional vibrations are received, and where they tend to be transformed into similar feeling in the receiving system, unless neutralized by other mental and emotional states in the person.

When we come to consider the apparatus by which is received the vibrations arising from what may be called "purely mental" operations of the brain, such as intellectual thought, constructive imagination, etc., we find a more specialized arrangement, as might be expected. There are several minor receiving points of mental vibrations, regarding which I do not consider it worth while to go into detail, because of the technical features involved. The principal apparatus for receiving thought vibrations of this kind is that which is known as the "pineal gland," which I shall now describe.

The pineal gland is a peculiar mass of nervous substance which is embedded in the human brain, in a position near the middle of the skull almost directly above the extreme top of the spinal column. It is shaped like a small cone; and is of a reddish-gray color. It lies in front of the cerebellum, and is attached to the floor of the third ventricle of the brain. It contains a small quantity of peculiar particles of gritty, sand-like substance, which are sometimes called "brain-sand." It derives its scientific name from its shape, which, as I have said, resembles a pine-cone. Physiologists are at sea regarding the function of this strange organ, and generally content themselves with the statement that "its functions are not understood." But occultists know that the pineal gland, with its peculiar arrangement of nerve-cell corpuscles, and its tiny grains of "brain-sand," is the physical telepathic receiving instrument. Students of wireless telegraphy have noticed a startling resemblance between the pineal gland and a part of the receiving instrument employed in wireless telegraphy.

The thought vibrations coming in contact with the nervous system of the receiving person, set up a peculiar vibration in the substance of the pineal gland and thus the first step in the transformation of these vibrations into thought-forms in the mind of the person is under way. The remainder of the process is too technical, both in the physiological as well as in the occult sense, to be taken up in detail at this place. The student will do well to get the idea of the workings of wireless telegraphy well fixed in his mind, for this will set up the right conception of the working of ordinary telepathy, without the necessity of complicated technical diagrams and descriptions.

And, now then, let us see what results from the sending forth and receiving of these mental and emotional waves of force and energy. It is a most interesting subject, I assure you. While the phenomena of the astral plane is probably more fascinating to the average student, I would impress upon you the importance of mastering the occult phenomena of the physical plane, before passing on to that of the higher planes.

In the first place, as all occultists know, each person is constantly surrounded with what has been called an "atmosphere" composed of mental and emotional vibrations which are emanated from his personality. The atmosphere of each person depends upon the general character of the thoughts and feelings of the person in question. Consequently, as no two persons are precisely alike in character, it follows that no two personal atmospheres are exactly alike. Each person has a psychic atmosphere of his or her own. These atmospheric vibrations do not extend very far from the presence of the person, and, consequently affect only those coming near to him.

In the same way, every group or crowd of persons has its own psychic atmosphere, composed of a blending of the individual psychic atmospheres of the persons composing the crowd, group or assemblage, and representing the general average of the thought and feelings of the crowd. There are no two group atmospheres exactly alike, for the reason that no two groups of persons, large or small, are exactly alike. Actors know that each audience which they face has its own psychic atmosphere, and the actors are affected by it. Preachers, lawyers, and speakers in general are quite aware of this fact, and freely admit it, though they may not be acquainted with the causes or laws governing the phenomena.

Following the same psychic law, it will be found that every town or large city, or even every small village or section of a larger town, will be found to have its own distinctive psychic atmosphere, which is very perceptible to strangers visiting the place, and which affect those who take up their residence in the place. In large cities, it has been noticed that every building has its own peculiar vibrations which arise from the general character of those occupying it. Different church buildings likewise reflect the character of the general habits of thought and feeling of those worshipping in them. Likewise, certain business streets have pleasant or unpleasant vibrations in their atmosphere, from the same causes. Every person recognizes the truth of these statements, though but few are able to account for the facts in a scientific manner.

The beginner in the study of psychic phenomena often asks how these things can be, when the thought which has occasioned the vibrations have long since passed away. The explanation is simple, when properly explained. It is something like this: just as heat remains in a room after the stove has ceased to throw out heat-waves, so do the vibrations of thought and feeling persist long after the thought or feeling has died away. Or, if you prefer a more material illustration, we may say that if a package of perfumery has been opened in a room, and then removed, the air will remain charged with the odor for a long time afterwards.

So, you see, the same principle applies in the case of psychic vibrations. The person carries around with him the general atmosphere of his characteristic mental and emotional vibrations. And, in the same way, the house, store, church, street, town, or city, etc., is permeated with the psychic vibrations of those who have frequented them. Nearly every one realizes the different feeling that impresses him when he enters a strange house, apartment, store or church. Each one has its own difference of psychic effect. And, so does each person create his or her psychic effect upon those coming in contact with him or her, or who comes into his or her presence or vicinity.

The next question asked by the thoughtful new student is this: If persons are constantly sending forth psychic vibrations, and if such vibrations persist for some time, why are we not overwhelmed with the force of them; and why are they not all so mixed up as to lose all their effect. I shall now answer this very important question.

In the first place, though we are constantly affected more or less by the multitude of psychic vibrations beating upon us, still the greater part of them do not consciously impress us. For an example, we have but to consider how few of the sounds or sights of a busy street are impressed upon our consciousness. We hear and see only a few of the things which attract our attention and interest. The rest are lost to us, although our eyes and ears receive them all. In the same way, we are impressed only by the stronger vibrations which reach us, and then only by those which we have attracted to ourselves, or which prove attractive to us by reason of our own likes and dislikes.

In the second place, the effect of certain thought vibrations is neutralized by the effect of the vibrations of thoughts of an opposite character. Just as a mixture of black and white produces the neutral color of grey, so do two currents of opposing thought vibrations tend to resolve themselves into a neutral vibration which has little or no effect upon those coming in contact with them. You may think of numerous correspondences to this in the world of material things. For instance, a mixture of very hot and very cold water, will produce a neutral lukewarm liquid, neither hot nor cold. In the same way, two things of opposing taste characteristics, when blended, will produce a neutral taste having but little effect upon one. The principle is universal, and is readily understood.

In the third place, there is that which we may call an "affinity" between thoughts and feelings of a similar character. Not only do the vibrations of similar thoughts tend to coalesce and combine; but, more than this, each one of us attracts to himself or herself the thought vibrations which are in general accord with corresponding thoughts in our own minds, or feelings in our own nature. Like attracts like. In the same way, the character of our thoughts and feelings act to repel thought or emotional vibrations of an opposite or inharmonious nature. As all occultists know, everyone draws thought vibrations in harmony with his or her own; and also repels thought vibrations of an inharmonious nature.

These are the general laws and principles governing the phenomena of this phase of telepathic vibrations. There is much more to be said on the subject, of course, but if you will note carefully the leading principles and laws of manifestation just mentioned, you will be able to reason correctly regarding any phase of this class of phenomena which may come before you for attention. Once you learn a general rule, the rest becomes merely a matter of application and interpretation. Let us now proceed to a consideration of other phases of the general subject of telepathic influence.

We now come to the phase of what may be called direct telepathy—that is where a thought is consciously, and more or less purposely, directed toward another person. We come across many interesting cases of this kind where persons find themselves thinking intently of certain other persons, and afterwards are told by the other persons that "I found myself thinking intently about you, at such and such a time," etc. In some of these cases it is difficult to determine which one started the thinking. Again, how often do we find ourselves thinking of a person, when all of a sudden the person comes into sight. Again, we think intently and earnestly about a certain question; and then, all of a sudden, other folks whom we meet begin talking to us about the same thing. These instances are too common to need more than a passing notice.

A little more purpose is displayed in that class of phenomena in which we intently wish that a certain person shall do a certain thing, and lo! we soon learn that that certain person has done it. A number of years ago, a popular writer wrote an article in which he mentioned what seemed to him to be a curious instance of some form of mental influence or telepathy. He said that he had found out that if he would sit down and carefully write a letter to some person from whom he had not heard for a long time, and then destroy the letter instead of sending it, he would be almost certain to receive a letter from that person within a few days. He did not attempt to account for the phenomenon, he merely called the attention of his readers to it. Many persons have followed the suggestion, often with very wonderful results. There is nothing miraculous, or supernatural about such occurrences. It is merely one phase of telepathy. The concentrated thought of the writer of the letter is directed toward the other person, and that person begins to think of the first one; then he thinks he will write to him; then he actually does write. Distance, space, and direction have no importance in this experiment—it is not necessary to even know where the second person is, in fact. There are often found persons so closely in psychic harmony with each other that they very often are able to ask questions and receive answers from each other, even though great distances separate them. Some particular times there is a better psychic harmony existing between the same persons than is found at other times. All this, of course, affects the success of the experiment. It is surprising what wonderful results along these lines may be obtained by almost any person of average intelligence, after a little careful, patient, conscientious practice.

But there have been phenomena obtained as the result of long series of careful experiments which are, in a way, even more wonderful than these somewhat less deliberate experiments just mentioned. I allude to the experiments of a number of earnest, careful scientific students, who surrounded themselves with every precaution against over-enthusiasm, fraud, and coincidence. Prominent among this class of investigations we find those conducted by the Society for Psychical Research, of England, which really established a firm basis for the work of other investigators who followed the general methods of the said society. In the following chapter, I shall give you a somewhat extended statement of the results of such investigations, because this information is important to every student of psychic phenomena, not only because it establishes a firm scientific basis for his studies and beliefs, but also because it gives him important information which he may apply in the course of his own experimental work.

I may mention that the investigations into the subject of telepathy, and kindred subjects, under the auspices of the society just mentioned, were conducted by men of careful scientific training and experience, and under the general supervision and approval of the officers of the society, among which have been numbered such eminent men as Prof. Henry Sidgwick, of Cambridge University; Prof. Balfour Stewart, a Fellow of the Royal Society of England; Rt. Hon. A.J. Balfour, the eminent English statesman; Prof. William James, the eminent American psychologist; Sir William Crookes, the great chemist and discoverer of physical laws, who invented the celebrated "Crookes' Tubes," without which the discovery of the X Rays, radio-activity, etc., would have been impossible; Frederick W.H. Myers, the celebrated explorer of the astral planes, and writer upon psychic phenomena; Sir Oliver Lodge, the popular English scientist; and other men of international reputation and high standing.

The character of these men at once gives the stamp of honesty and scientific accuracy to all the work of the society.

In order that you may understand the spirit which animated these scientific investigators in their work of the exploration of this new and strange region of Nature, I ask you to carefully read the following words of the presidential address of Sir William Crookes, before the Royal Society, at Bristol, England, in 1898. Remember, please, that this address was made before an assemblage of distinguished scientists, many of them rank materialists and, quite skeptical of all occult phenomena—this was nearly twenty years ago, remember. Sir William Crookes, facing this gathering, as its president, said:

"Were I now introducing for the first time these inquiries to the world of science, I should choose a starting point different from that of old (where we formerly began). It would be well to begin with Telepathy; with that fundamental law, as I believe it to be, that thoughts and images may be transferred from one mind to another without the agency of the recognized organs of sense—that knowledge may enter the human mind without being communicated in any hitherto known or recognized ways. * * * If telepathy takes place, we have two physical facts—the physical change in the brain of A, the suggestor, and the analogous physical change in the brain of B, the recipient of the suggestion. Between these two physical events there must exist a train of physical causes. * * * It is unscientific to call in the aid of mysterious agencies, when with every fresh advance in knowledge it is shown that either vibrations have powers and attributes abundantly able to any demand—even the transmission of thought.

"It is supposed by some physiologists that the essential cells of nerves do not actually touch, but are separated by a narrow gap which widens in sleep while it narrows almost to extinction during mental activity. This condition is so singularly like a Branly or Lodge coherer (a device which led to the discovery of wireless telegraphy) as to suggest a further analogy. The structure of brain and nerve being similar, it is conceivable that there may be present masses of such nerve coherers in the brain, whose special function it may be to receive impulses brought from without, through the connecting sequence of ether waves of appropriate order of magnitude.

"Roentgen has familiarized us with an order of vibrations of extreme minuteness as compared with the smallest waves with which we have hitherto been acquainted: and there is no reason to suppose that we have here reached the limit of frequency. It is known that the action of thought is accompanied by certain molecular movements in the brain, and here we have physical vibrations capable from their extreme minuteness of acting direct upon individual molecules, while their rapidity approaches that of internal and external movements of the atoms themselves. A formidable range of phenomena must be scientifically sifted before we effectually grasp a faculty so strange, so bewildering, and for ages so inscrutable, as the direct action of mind upon mind.

"In the old Egyptian days, a well known inscription was carved over the portal of the Temple of Isis: 'I am whatever has been, is, or ever will be; and my veil no man hath yet lifted.' Not thus do modern seekers after truth confront Nature—the word that stands for the baffling mysteries of the Universe. Steadily, unflinchingly, we strive to pierce the inmost heart of Nature, from what she is to reconstruct what she has been, and to prophesy what she shall be. Veil after veil we have lifted, and her face grows more beautiful, august and wonderful, with every barrier that is withdrawn."

You will notice that this address made nearly twenty years ago, and from the standpoint of physical science is in full accord with the ideas of occultism as old as the hills. And yet, the speaker had worked out the idea independently. He also investigated higher forms of psychic phenomena, with results that startled the world. But, you will notice that he does not attempt to give any other than purely physical laws the credit for the ordinary phenomena of telepathy. And he was thoroughly right in this, as we have seen. He escaped the common error of confusing physical-sense phenomena with the phenomena of the astral-senses. Each plane has its own phenomena—and each class is surely wonderful enough. And, again, remember that both physical and astral phenomena are purely natural; there is no need for seeking any supernatural agencies to account for these natural facts.

LESSON - IV

SCIENTIFIC TELEPATHY

The investigators of the Society for Psychical Research, of England, started by giving a broad definition of Telepathy, as follows: "Telepathy is the communication of impressions of any kind from one mind to another, independently of the recognized channels of sense." They took the rational position that the actual distance between the projector and the recipient of the telepathic message is not material; and that all that is required is such a separation of the two persons that no known operation of the senses can bridge the space between them. They wisely held that telepathy between two persons in the same room is as much telepathy as when the two persons are located at opposite sides of the world.

The investigators then ruled out all instances of thought-transmission in which there was even the slightest muscular contact between the projector and the recipient. They held that though there might be genuine telepathy in such cases, nevertheless, there was always the possibility of fraud or collusion, or of unconscious muscular action on the part of the projector. They demanded absolute and actual separation of the two persons, in order that their experiments might be above suspicion. They were wise in this, for while there is undoubtedly a psychic communication in the cases in which there is the slight physical connection between the two persons (as I shall point out to you a little further on), still the element of doubt or suspicion must be entirely eliminated from a scientific test, in order to render it valuable and valid.

They, therefore, confined their investigations in Telepathy to the two following classes, viz.: (1) where actions are performed without physical contact with the person willing; and (2) where some number, word, or card is guessed apparently without any of the ordinary means of communication. The investigators recognized the possibility that in the first of the above-mentioned two classes of experiments there is a possibility of suspicion of collusion, fraud, or unconscious suggestion, in the matter of the motion of the eyes of the party, or some member of it, which might be seized upon, perhaps unconsciously, by the recipient, and used to guide him to the object which was being thought of by the projector or the party. They sought to obviate this difficulty by blindfolding the percipient, and by placing non-conductors of sound over his ears. But, finally, they came to the conclusion that even these precautions might not prove sufficient; and, accordingly, they devoted their attention to the second class of experiments, in which all ordinary means of communication between projector and recipient were impossible. They took the additional precautions of limiting their circle to a small number of investigators of scientific reputations, and well known to each other, always avoiding a promiscuous company for obvious reasons.

One of the earliest series of investigations by these special committees of investigators was that of the family of the Rev. A.M. Creery, in Derbyshire, England. The children of this family had acquired a reputation in what was known as the "guessing game," in which one of the children, previously placed outside of the room, then returned to the room and attempted to "guess" the name or location of some object agreed upon by the party during her absence. The results were very interesting, and quite satisfactory, and have frequently been referred to in works on the subject written since that time. I think it well to give the results of this series of experiments in some little detail, for they form a basis for experiments on the part of those who read these lessons.

Prof. W.F. Barrett, Professor of Physics in the Royal College of Science for Ireland, conducted the most of the experiments. The report to the Society says: "We began by selecting the simplest objects in the room; then chose names of towns, people, dates, cards out of a pack, lines from different poems, etc., in fact, any thing or series of ideas that those present could keep in their minds steadily. The children seldom made a mistake. I have seen seventeen cards chosen by myself named right in succession without any mistake. We soon found that a great deal depended on the steadiness with which the ideas were kept before the minds of the thinkers, and upon the energy with which they willed the ideas to pass. I may say that this faculty is not by any means confined to the members of one family; it is much more general than we imagine. To verify this conclusion, I invited two of a neighbor's children to join us in our experiments, with excellent results."

The report gives the methods of the experiments, as follows: "The inquiry has taken place partly in Mr. Creery's house, and partly in lodgings, or at a hotel occupied by some of our number. Having selected at random one child, whom we desired to leave the room and wait at some distance, we would choose a pack of cards, or write on a piece of paper a name of a number which occurred to us at the moment. Generally, but not always, this was shown to the members of the family present in the room; but no one member was always present, and we were sometimes entirely alone. We then recalled the child, one of us always assuring himself that, when the door was suddenly opened, she was at a considerable distance, though this was usually a superfluity of caution, as our habit was to avoid all utterances of what was chosen. On re-entering, she stood—sometimes turned by us with her face toward the wall, oftener with her eyes directed toward the ground, and usually close to us and remote from the family—for a period of silence varying from a few seconds to a minute, till she called out to us some number, card, or whatever it might be."

In the first experiments, in "guessing" the name of objects, the child guessed correctly six out of fourteen. She then guessed correctly the name of small objects held in the hands of one of the committee—five times out of six. She guessed fictitious names chosen by the committee—five out of ten, at the first trial. The committee then tested her by writing down the name of some object in the house, fixed at random, and then, after all had thought intently of the thing, they sent for the child and bade her try to find the thing thought of, the thought-concentration of course continuing during the search. The result is thus reported: "In this way I wrote down, among other things, a hair-brush—it was brought; an orange—it was brought; a wine-glass—it was brought; an apple—it was brought; and so on, until many objects had been selected and found by the child."

Passing over the details of many other experiments we find that the following remarkable results were obtained by the committee: "Altogether, three hundred and eighty-two trials were made in this series. In the case of letters of the alphabet, of cards, and of numbers of two figures, the chances of success on a first trial would naturally be 25 to 1, 52 to 1, and 89 to 1, respectively; in the case of surnames they would of course be infinitely greater. Cards were far most frequently employed, and the odds in their case may be taken as a fair medium sample, according to which, out of a whole series of three hundred and eighty-two trials, the average number of successes at the first attempt by an ordinary guesser would be seven and one-third. Of our trials, one hundred and twenty-seven were successes on the first attempt, fifty-six on the second, nineteen on the third—MAKING TWO HUNDRED AND TWO, OUT OF A POSSIBLE THREE HUNDRED AND EIGHTY-TWO!" Think of this, while the law of averages called for only seven and one-third successes at first trial, the children obtained one hundred and twenty-seven, which, given a second and third trial, they raised to two hundred and two! You see, this takes the matter entirely out of the possibility of coincidence or mathematical probability.

But this was not all. Listen to the further report of the committee on this point: "The following was the result of one of the series. The thing selected was divulged to none of the family, and five cards running were named correctly on a first trial. The odds against this happening once in a series were considerably over a million to one. There were other similar batches, the two longest runs being eight consecutive guesses, once with cards, and once with names; where the adverse odds in the former case were over one hundred and forty-two millions to one; and in the other, something incalculably greater." The opinion of eminent mathematicians who have examined the above results is that the hypothesis of mere coincidence is practically excluded in the scientific consideration of the matter. The committee calls special attention to the fact that in many of the most important tests none of the Creery family were cognizant of the object selected, and that, therefore, the hypothesis of fraud or collusion is absolutely eliminated. The committee naturally came to the conclusion that the phenomena was genuine and real telepathy.

Prof. Balfour Stewart, LL.D., F.R.S., who was present at some of these experiments, though not a member of the committee, expressed great amazement at some of the results. He reports: "The thought-reader was outside a door. The object or thing thought of was written on paper and silently handed to the company in the room. The thought reader was then called in, and in the course of a minute the answer was given. Definite objects in the room, for instance, were first thought of, and in the majority of the cases the answers were correct. Then numbers were thought of, and the answers were generally right, though, of course, there were some cases of error. The names of towns were thought of, and a good many of these were right. Then fancy names were thought of. I was asked to think of certain fancy names, and mark them down and hand them round to the company. I thought of and wrote on paper, 'Blue-beard,' 'Tom Thumb,' 'Cinderella.' and the answers were all correct!"

The committee also conducted a number of experiments with other recipients, with very satisfactory results. Colors were correctly guessed with a percentage of successes quite beyond the average or probable number. Names of towns in all parts of the world, were correctly "guessed" by certain recipients with a wonderful degree of success. But, probably most wonderful of all, was the correct reproduction of diagrams of geometrical and other figures and shapes. In one case, the recipient, in a series of nine trials, succeeded in drawing them all correctly, except that he frequently reversed them, making the upper-side down, and the right-hand side to the left. The Society, has published these reproduced diagrams in its Illustrated reports, and they have convinced the most skeptical of critics. Some of the diagrams were quite complicated, unusual, and even grotesque, and yet they were reproduced with marvelous accuracy, not in a hesitating manner, but deliberately and continuously, as if the recipient were actually copying a drawing in full sight. Similar results have been obtained by other investigators who have followed the lead of these original ones.

So you see, the seal of scientific authority has been placed upon the phenomena of telepathy. It is no longer in the realm of the supernatural or uncanny. As Camille Flammarion, the eminent French scientist, has said: "The action of one mind upon another at a distance—the transmission of thought, mental suggestion, communication at a distance—all these are not more extraordinary than the action of the magnet on iron, the influence of the moon on the sea, the transportation of the human voice by electricity, the revolution of the chemical constituents of a star by the analysis of its light, or, indeed, all the wonders of contemporary science. Only these psychic communications are of a more elevated kind, and may serve to put us on the track of a knowledge of human nature. What is certain is: That telepathy can and ought to be henceforth considered by Science as an incontestable reality; that minds are able to act upon each other without the intervention of the senses; that psychic force exists, though its nature is yet unknown. * * * We say that this force is of a psychic order, and not physical, or physiological, or chemical, or mechanical, because it produces and transmits ideas and thoughts, and because it manifests itself without the co-operation of our senses, soul to soul, mind to mind."

In addition to investigating the above mentioned classes of telepathic phenomena, the English Society for Psychical Research investigated many remarkable cases of a somewhat higher phase of telepathy. They took down the stories told by persons deemed responsible, and then carefully examined, and cross-examined other witnesses to the strange phenomena. The record of these experiments, and investigations, fill a number of good sized volumes of the Society's reports, which are well worth reading by all students of the subject. They may be found in the libraries of nearly any large city. I shall, however, select a number of the most interesting of the cases therein reported, to give my students an idea of the character of the phenomena so investigated and found genuine by the committees having this class of telepathy under investigation.

An interesting case of spontaneous telepathy is that related by Dr. Ede, as follows: "There is a house about a half-mile from my own, inhabited by some ladies, friends of our family. They have a large alarm bell outside their house. One night I awoke suddenly and said to my wife: 'I am sure I hear Mrs. F's alarm bell ringing.' After listening for some time, we heard nothing, and I went to sleep again. The next day Mrs. F. called upon my wife and said to her: 'We were wishing for your husband last night, for we were alarmed by thieves. We were all up, and I was about to pull the alarm bell, hoping that he would hear it, saying to my daughters, "I am sure it will soon bring Dr. Ede," but we did not ring it.' My wife asked what time this had happened, and Mrs. F. said that it was about half past one. That was the time I awoke thinking that I heard the bell."

In this case there was manifested simply ordinary physical plane telepathy. Had the bell actually been rung, and heard psychically, it would have been a case of astral plane hearing, known as clairaudience. As it was, merely the thought in the mind of Mrs. F., and her strong idea to ring the bell, caused a transmission of thought waves which struck Dr. Ede with great force and awakened him. This case is interesting because it is typical of many cases of a similar nature within the experience of many persons. It is seen that a strong feeling, or excitement, accompanied by a strong desire or wish to summon another person, tends to give great power and effect to the thought waves emitted. They strike the mind of the recipient like the sudden ringing of an alarm clock bell.

Another interesting case is that of two ladies, both well known to members of the committee, and vouched for as of strict veracity. This case is unusual for the reason that two different persons received the thought-waves at the same time. Here is an abridgment of the case: "Lady G. and her sister had been spending the evening with their mother, who was in her usual health and spirits when they left her. In the middle of the night the sister awoke in her fright and said to her husband: 'I must go to my mother at once; do order the carriage. I am sure that she is taken ill.' On the way to her mother's house, where two roads meet, she saw Lady G.'s carriage approaching. When they met each asked the other why she was there. They both related the same experience and impression. When they reached their mother's house, they found that she was dying, and had expressed an earnest wish to see them."

Another case of a similar nature is this: "At the siege of Mooltan, Major General R., then adjutant of his regiment, was severely wounded and supposed himself to be dying. He requested that his ring be taken off his finger and sent to his wife. At the same time his wife was at Ferozepore, one hundred and fifty miles distant, lying on her bed, in a state half way between waking and sleeping. She saw her husband being taken off the field, and heard his voice saying: 'Take this ring off my finger, and send it to my wife.'"

This case bears the marks of very strong telepathy, but also has a suspicious resemblance to clairvoyance accompanied by clairaudience. Or perhaps it is a combination of both telepathy and clairvoyance. It is impossible to determine which, in absence of more detailed information. The message of persons dying, or believing themselves to be approaching death, are frequently very strong, for certain reasons well known to occultists. But there is nothing supernatural about the phenomena, and in most cases it is merely a case of strong telepathy.

The Society also reports the following interesting case: "A. was awake, and strongly willed to make himself known to two friends who at that time (one o'clock in the morning) were asleep. When he met them a few days afterward, they both told him that at one o'clock they had awakened under the impression that he was in their room. The experience was so vivid that they could not go to sleep for some time, and looked at their watches to note the time." Cases of this kind are quite common, and many experimenters have had equally good results with this phase of thought transference. You will remember that there is no actual projection of the astral body, in most of these cases, but merely a strong impression caused by concentrated thought.

Another interesting case is that of the late Bishop Wilberforce, and is recorded in his biography, as follows: The Bishop was in his library at Cuddleson, with three or four of his clergy with him at the same table. The Bishop suddenly raised his hand to his head, and exclaimed: "I am certain that something has happened to one of my sons." It afterwards transpired that just at that time his eldest son's foot was badly crushed by an accident on board his ship, the son being at sea. The Bishop himself recorded the circumstance in a letter to Miss Noel, saying: "It is curious that at the time of his accident I was so possessed with the depressing consciousness of some evil having befallen my son, Herbert, that at the last, I wrote down that I was unable to shake off the impression that something had happened to him, and noted this down for remembrance." There is nothing unusual about this case, for it has been duplicated in the experience of many persons. Its chief importance lies in the fact that it is recorded by a man of wide reputation and high standing, and also that the Bishop had taken the precaution to note down the thing at the time, instead of merely recalling it after he had heard of the accident.

You will notice that in many cases of this kind the phenomenon closely approaches the aspect of true clairvoyance, or astral sensing. In some cases there appears to be a blending of both telepathy and astral clairvoyance. In fact, there is but very little difference between the highest phases of ordinary telepathy, and the more common phases of clairvoyance. Here, as in many other cases of Nature's forces, there seems to be a gradual blending, rather than a sharp dividing line between the two classes of phenomena. Moreover, the student developing his telepathic powers will frequently find that he is beginning to unfold at least occasional flashes of clairvoyance.

In the case of telepathy, the recipient merely senses what is in the mind of the projector. In some cases a picture in the mind of the projector may be seen by the recipient, and may thus be mistaken for a case of pure clairvoyance. But, in investigating closely, it will be found that the real scene was slightly different from the impression, in which case it shows that the impression was simply telepathic. Clairvoyant vision shows the scene as it really is, or rather as the physical eye of the recipient would have seen it. The astral sight really sees the scene, and does not merely receive the mental impression of the projector. The first is original seeing; the second, merely a reproduction of images already in the mind of the projector, and colored by his personality, etc.

In the next lesson, I shall give you a number of exercises and methods designed to develop your telepathic powers. You will find the practice of these most interesting and entertaining, and at the same time most instructive. You will find that as you practice the exercises given therein, you will become more and more adept and proficient in producing telepathic phenomena. From the lower stages, you will be able to proceed to the higher. And, in time, you will be surprised to find that almost unconsciously you have passed into the stage in which you will have at least occasional manifestations of clairvoyance, psychometry, etc.

In fact, there is no better way known to practical occultists to develop in a student the powers of clairvoyance than just this method of starting the student with the exercises designed to develop the telepathic power. It has been found by centuries of experience that the student who develops telepathic power, in a systematic way, will gradually unfold and evolve the clairvoyant and psychometric power. It constitutes the first rungs on the ladder of psychic development.

Of course, under the head of clairvoyance, etc., you will be given methods and exercise designed to develop clairvoyant powers—some of them very valuable and effective methods, at that. But, notwithstanding this, I feel that I should impress upon you the importance of laying a firm foundation for such instruction, by developing yourself first along the lines of telepathic power. Such a course will not only keenly sharpen your powers of receptivity to such vibrations as you may wish to receive; but it will also train your mind in the direction of translating, interpreting, and recording such impressions when received.

You must remember that proficiency in a mental art is attained only by means of training the attention to concentrate upon the task. It is the same way in clairvoyance and psychometry. Telepathy trains your attention to concentrate upon the reception of impressions, and to hold them firmly and clearly in consciousness. The result is that when you really develop clairvoyant receptivity, your attention has already been trained to do the necessary work. I need not tell you what an advantage this gives you over the clairvoyant who has not received this training, for your own good common sense will assure you of it.

So, now for our training in telepathy—not only for itself, but also as a means of preparing for the higher stages.

LESSON - V

MIND READING AND BEYOND

The simpler forms of telepathic phenomena have received the name "Mind Reading" and by some have been regarded as something not quite within the class of real telepathy. This last impression has been heightened by the fact that there has been offered the public many spectacular exhibitions of pseudo mind-reading, that is to say, imitation or counterfeit mind-reading, in which the result has been obtained by trickery, collusion, or clever artifice. But, notwithstanding this fact, genuine mind-reading is actually a phase of true telepathy.

What is generally known as mind-reading may be divided into two classes, as follows: (1) where there is an actual physical contact between the projector and the receiver; and (2) where there is no actual physical contact, but where there is a close relation in space between the two parties, as in the case of the "willing game." In the first class belong all cases in which the projector touches the recipient, or at least is connected with him by a material object. In the second class belong those cases in which the recipient seeks to find an object which is being thought of by either a single projector, or by a number of persons in the same room. You will notice that both of these classes were omitted from the experiments of the Society for Psychical Research, because of the possibility of fraud or collusion. But, nevertheless, the student will do well to acquire proficiency in manifesting this form of telepathy, not alone for its own sake, but, also, because it naturally leads to higher development.

In the case of the first class of mind-reading namely, that in which actual physical contact is had between the projector and the recipient, there has been a disposition on the part of some authorities to explain the whole matter by the theory of unconscious muscular impulse of the projector; but those who have carefully studied this subject, and who have themselves performed the feats of this class of mind-reading, know that there is far more than this to it. Those familiar with the subject know that there is a decided transference of thought-waves from the projector to the recipient, and that the latter actually "feels" the same as they strike upon his mental receiving apparatus. The whole difference between this and the higher forms of telepathy is that in this the thought-currents generally run along the wires of the nervous system, instead of leaping across the space between the two persons.

It is known to all who have conducted this class of experiments, that at times there will be experienced a change or shifting in the transmission of the thought-currents. For a time, the thought-waves will be felt flowing in along the nerves of the hands and arms when, all of a sudden this will cease, and there will be experienced the passage of the current direct from brain to brain. It is impossible to describe this feeling in mere words, to those who have never experienced it. But those to whom it has once been manifested will recognize at once just what I mean by this statement. It is a different sensation from any other in the experience of a human being, and must actually be experienced to be understood. The nearest analogy I can offer is that feeling experienced by the person when a forgotten name for which he has vainly sought, suddenly flashes or leaps into his consciousness—it is felt to come from somewhere outside of the conscious field. Well, in the case of the thought-current the feeling is much the same, only there is a fuller sense of the "outsideness" of the source of the thought.

In order to make you understand the distinction between the two classes of mind-reading more clearly, I will say that you may think of one as akin to the ordinary telegraphy over wires; and of the other as akin to wireless telegraphy. It is the same force in both cases, the difference being simply one of the details of transmission. Fix this idea firmly in your mind, and you will have no trouble in always having the right conception of any kind of case of mind-reading, or telepathy. But, you must remember, there are cases in which there is a combination of both methods of transmission, either simultaneously, or else shifting and changing from one to the other.

I will here remind the student that he will learn more by a half-dozen actual experiments in mind-reading, than he will by reading a dozen books on the subject. It is very good to read the books in order to get the correct theory well fixed in mind, and also in order to learn the best methods as taught by those who have had a wide experience in the subject; but the real "how" of the matter is learned only through actual experience. So, I shall now give you advice and instructions concerning actual experimental work.

You, the student, should begin by making yourself a good recipient—that is a good "mind reader," allowing others to play the part of projector. Later on, you may play the part of projector, if you so desire, but the real "fine work" is done by the recipient, and, for that reason that is the part you should learn to play by frequent rehearsals.

I advise you to begin your experiments with friends who are in sympathy with you, and who are interested in the subject. Avoid particularly all early experiments with uncongenial or unsympathetic persons; and avoid as you would a pestilence all those who are antagonistic either to yourself or to the general subject of telepathy and kindred subjects. As you must make yourself especially "sensitive" in order to successfully conduct a mind-reading test, you will find yourself particularly susceptible to the mental attitude of those around you at such times, and therefore should surround yourself only with those who are congenial and sympathetic.

You will find that there is a great difference between the several persons whom you "try out" as projectors. Some will be more "en rapport" with you than are others who may be equally good friends. "En rapport," you know, means "in vibrational harmony." When two persons are en rapport with each other, they are like two wireless telegraphic instruments perfectly attuned to each other. In such cases there are obtained the very best results. You will soon learn to distinguish the degree of en rapport conditions between yourself and different persons—you soon learn to "feel" this condition. In the beginning, it will be well for you to try several persons, one after the other, in your mind-reading experiments, in order to pick out the best one, and also to learn the "feel" of the different degrees of en rapport condition.

Even in cases of persons in whom the en rapport conditions are good, it is well to establish a rhythmic unison between you. This is done by both you and the person breathing in rhythmic unison a few moments. Begin by counting "one-two-three-four," like the slow ticking of a large clock. Have the other person join with you in so counting, until your minds both work in the same rhythmic time. Then you should have him breathe in unison with you, making a mental count with you at the same time, so that you will "breathe together." Count (mentally) "one-two-three-four," as you inhale; the "one-two," holding the breath; and, then "one-two-three-four," exhaling or breathing-out. Try this several times, and, you will find that you have established a rhythmic unison between yourself and the other person. In the progress of an experiment, if you should find that the conditions are not as good as might be desired, you will do well to pause for a few moments and re-establish the proper rhythmic harmony by this method of harmonious rhythmic breathing.

Begin by having the projector select some prominent object in the room, a chair, or table for instance. Then have him take your left hand in his right hand. Raise your left hand, held in his right hand, to your forehead; then close your eyes and remain passive a few moments. Have him concentrate his mind intently on the selected object—and will that you should move toward it. Have him think of nothing else except that object, and to will you to move toward it, with all his power. Close your eyes, and quiet your mind, opening your consciousness to every mental impression that he may send you. Instruct him to think not merely "chair," for instance, but rather "there—go there." The main thought in his mind must be that of direction. He must will that you move toward that chair.

After a moment or two, you will begin to feel a vague, general impulse to move your feet. Obey the impulse. Take a few slow steps in any direction that seems easy to you. Sometimes this will take you in an opposite direction from that of the chair, but it will "get you going," and you will soon begin to feel that the direction is "all wrong," and will begin to be mentally pulled in the right direction. You will have to actually experience this feeling, before you will fully understand just what I mean.

After some little practice, you will begin to feel quite distinctly the mental direction, or will-force, of the projector, which will seem to tell you to "come this way—now stop—now turn a little to the right—now a little to the left—now stop where you are, and put out your right hand—lower your hand—move your hand a little to the right—that's it, now you have got it all right." You will soon learn to distinguish between the "no, that's wrong" thought, and the "that's right" one; and between the "go on," and the "come on" one. By making yourself completely passive, and receptive and obedient to the thought and will-impulses of the projector, you will soon act like a ship under the influence of the rudder in the hand of the projector.

After you have attained proficiency in receiving the mental impressions and directions, you will find yourself attracted or drawn, like a piece of steel to the magnet, toward the object selected. It will sometimes seem as if you were being moved to it even against your own will—and as if someone else were actually moving your feet for you. Sometimes the impulse will come so strong that you will actually rush ahead of the projector, dragging him along with you, instead of having him a little in advance, or by your side. It is all a matter of practice.

You will soon discover the great difference between different projectors. Some of them will be in perfect en rapport condition with you, while others will fail to get into tune with you. Some projectors do not seem to know what is required of them, and usually forget to "will" you to the object. It helps sometimes to tell them that the whole thing depends upon their will power, and that the stronger their will is, the easier it is for you to find the thing. This puts them on their mettle, and makes them use their will more vigorously.

You will soon learn to recognize that peculiar feeling of "all right," that comes when you finally stand in front of the desired object. Then you begin to move your right hand up and down and around, until you get the right "feel" about that also, when you should place your hand on the place which seems to attract you most. You will find that the hand is just as responsive to the mental force, as are the feet. You will soon learn to distinguish between the mental signals: "up," "down," "to the right," "to the left," "stop now, you're right," etc. I cannot tell you just the difference—you must learn to "feel" them, and you will soon become expert in this. It is like learning to skate, run an automobile, operate a typewriter or anything else—all a matter of exercise and practice. But it is astonishing how rapidly one may learn; and how, at times, one seems to progress by great leaps and bounds. Now I shall give you the different stages or steps, which you will do well to follow in your exercises, progressing from the more simple to the more complex—but be sure to thoroughly master the simple ones, before you pass on to the more complex one. Be honest and strict with yourself—make yourself "pass the examination" before promotion, in each and every step.

1. **Locations.** Begin by finding particular locations in a room; corners, alcoves, doors, etc.
2. **Large Objects.** Then begin to find large objects, such as tables, chairs, book-cases, etc.
3. **Small Objects.** Then proceed to find small objects, such as books on a table, sofa-cushions, ornaments, paper-knives, etc. Gradually work down to very small objects, such as scarf-pins, articles of jewelry, pocket-knives, etc.
4. **Concealed Objects.** Then proceed to find small objects that have been concealed under other objects, such as a pocket-book beneath a sofa-cushion, etc.; or a key in a book; or a key under a rug, etc.
5. **Minute Objects.** Then proceed to discover very small objects, either concealed or else placed in an inconspicuous place, such as a pin stuck in the wall, etc.; or a small bean under a vase, etc.

The public performers of mind reading vary the above by sensational combinations, but you will readily see that these are but ingenious arrangements of the above general experiments, and that no new principle is involved. As these lessons are designed for serious study and experiment, and not for sensational public performances, I shall not enter into this phase of the subject in these pages. The student who understands the general principles, and is able to perform the above experiments successfully, will have no difficulty in reproducing the genuine feats of the public mind readers, by simply using his ingenuity in arranging the stage-effects, etc. Among other things, he will find that he will be able to obtain results by interposing a third person between the projector and himself; or by using a short piece of wire to connect himself and the projector. Drawing pictures on a blackboard, or writing out names on a slate, by means of thought direction, are simply the result of a fine development of the power of finding the small article—the impulse to move the hand in a certain direction comes in precisely the same way. The public driving feats of the professional mind-reader are but a more complicated form of the same general principle—the impression of "direction" once obtained, the rest is a mere matter of detail. The opening of the combination of a safe, though requiring wonderful proficiency on the part of the operator, is simply an elaboration of the "direction" movement.

Some recipients are, of course, far more proficient than are others; but each and every person—any person of average intelligence—will be able to secure more or less proficiency in these experiments, provided that patience and practice are employed. There is no such thing as an absolute failure possible to anyone who will proceed intelligently, and will practice sufficiently. Sometimes, after many discouraging attempts, the whole thing will flash into one's mind at once, and after that there will be little or no trouble. If you are able to witness the demonstrations of some good mind-reader, professional or amateurs it will help you to "catch the knack" at once.

You will find that these experiments will tend to greatly and rapidly develop your psychic receptivity in the direction of the higher phases of psychic phenomena. You will be surprised to find yourself catching flashes or glimpses of higher telepathy, or even clairvoyance. I would advise every person wishing to cultivate the higher psychic faculties, to begin by perfecting himself or herself in these simpler forms of mind-reading. Besides the benefits obtained, the practice proves very interesting, and opens many doors to pleasant social entertainment. But, never allow the desire for social praise or popularity, in these matters, to spoil you for serious investigation and experiment.

The Second Step of Development. The student, having perfected himself in the experiments along the lines of the first class of mind-reading, viz., where there is no actual physical contact between the projector and recipient, but where there is a close relation in space between the two.

Now, the thoughtful student will naturally wish to ask a question here, something like this: "You have told us that there is no real difference between telepathy at a great distance, and that in which there is only the slightest difference in the position of the projector and recipient, providing, always, that there is no actual physical contact. This being so, why your insistence upon the 'close relation in space' just mentioned?—what is the reason for this nearness?" Well, it is like this: While there is no distinction of space in true telepathy, still in experiments such as I shall now describe, the physical nearness of the projector enables him to concentrate more forcibly, and also gives confidence to the new beginner in receiving mind-currents. The benefit is solely that of the psychological effect upon the minds of the two persons, and has nothing to do with the actual power of the telepathic waves. It is much easier for a person to concentrate his thought and will upon a person in actual physical sight before him, than upon one out of sight. And, likewise, the recipient finds himself more confident and at ease when in the actual physical of the person sending the thoughts and will power. That is all there is to it. When the persons have acquired familiarity with projecting and receiving, then this obstacle is overcome, and long distances have no terror for them.

The best way for the student to start in on this class of mind-reading, is for him to experiment occasionally while performing his physical contact mind-reading experiments. For instance, while engaged in searching for an object let him disengage his hand from that of the projector for a moment or so, and then endeavor to receive the impressions without contact. (This should be done only in private experiments, not in public ones.) He will soon discover that he is receiving thought impulses in spite of the lack of physical contact—faint, perhaps, but still perceptible. A little practice of this kind will soon convince him that he is receiving the mental currents direct from brain to brain. This effect will be increased if he arranges to have several persons concentrate their thoughts and will power upon him during the experiment. From this stage, he will gradually develop into the stage of the Willing Game.

The Willing Game, quite popular in some circles, is played by one person (usually blind-folded) being brought into the room in which a number of persons have previously agreed upon some object to be found by him, they concentrating their thought firmly upon the object. The audience should be taught to not only to think but also to actively "will" the progress of the recipient from the start to the finish of the hunt. They should "will" him along each step of his journey, and then "will" his hand to the object itself wherever it be hidden.

An adept in the receiving end of the Willing Game will be able to perform all the experiments that I have just pointed out to you in the contact mind-reading class. In the Willing Game, you must remember that there is no taking hold of hands or any other form of physical contact between projector and recipient. The transmission of the mental currents must be direct, from brain to brain. Otherwise, the two classes of experiments are almost identical. There is the same "willing" toward the object on the part of the projectors, and the same passive obedience of the recipient. All the difference is that the current now passes over the ether of space, as in the case of the wireless message, instead of over the wires of the nervous system of the two persons.

The next step is that of "guessing" the name of things thought of by the party. I can give you no better directions than those followed by the investigators in the Creery children, as related in a preceding chapter of this book. When you become sufficiently proficient in this class of mind-reading, you should be able to reproduce every experiment there mentioned, with at least a fair degree of success. It is all a matter of patience, perseverance and practice.

After you have become very proficient in this class of experiments, you may begin to try experiments at "long distance," that is where the projector is out of your physical presence. It makes no difference whether the distance be merely that between two adjoining rooms, or else of miles of space. At first, however, nearness adds confidence in the majority of cases. Confidence once gained, the distance may be lengthened indefinitely, without impairing the success of the experiments. The long distance experiments may consist either of the receiving of single words, names, etc., or else distinct, clear messages or ideas. Some find it no more difficult to reproduce simile geometrical designs, such as circles, squares, triangles, etc., than to reproduce words or ideas.

In long distance experiments, it is well for the projector to write down the word or thought he wishes to transmit, and for the recipient to write down the impressions he receives. These memoranda will serve as a record of progress, and will, moreover, give a scientific value to the experiments.

Some experimentors have been quite successful in experiments along the lines of Automatic Writing from living persons, produced by means of long distance telepathy. In these cases the recipient sits passively at the hour agreed upon for the experiment, and the projector concentrates intently upon a sentence, or several sentences, one word at a time—at the same time "willing" the other person to write the word. The famous investigator of psychic phenomena, the late W.T. Stead, editor of a London newspaper, who went down on the "Titanic," was very successful in experiments of this kind. His written records of these are very interesting and instructive.

You will, of course, understand that in all cases of long distance telepathic experiments there should be an understanding between the two persons regarding the time and duration of the experiment, so as to obtain the best results. Personally, however, I have known of some very excellent results in which the receiving of the message occurred several hours after the sending—thus showing that telepathy is in a measure independent of time, as well as of space. But, as a rule, the best results are obtained when the two persons "sit" simultaneously.

Do not rest content with accepting the reports of others regarding these things. Try them for yourself. You will open up a wonderful world of new experiences for yourself. But, remember always, you must proceed step by step, perfecting yourself at each step before proceeding to the next.

LESSON - VI

CLAIRVOYANT PSYCHOMETRY

The word "clairvoyance" means "clear seeing." In its present usage it covers a wide field of psychic phenomena; and is used by different writers to designate phases of psychic phenomena differing widely from each other. The student is apt to become confused when he meets these apparently conflicting definitions and usages. In the glossary of the Society for Psychical Research, the term is defined as: "The faculty or act of perceiving, as though visually, with some coincidental truth, some distant scene; it is used sometimes, but hardly properly, for transcendental vision, or the perception of beings regarded as on another plane of existence."

Mrs. Henry Sidgwick, a distinguished writer on the subject of psychic phenomena, in one of her reports to the Society for Psychical Research, says: "The word clairvoyant is often used very loosely and with widely different meanings. I denote by it a faculty of acquiring supernormally, but not by reading the minds of persons present, a knowledge of facts such as we normally acquire by the use of our senses. I do not limit it to knowledge that would normally be acquired by the sense of sight, nor do I limit it to a knowledge of present facts. A similar knowledge of the past, and if necessary, of future facts may be included. On the other hand, I exclude the mere faculty of seeing apparitions or visions, which is sometimes called clairvoyance."

The above definitive explanation of the term clairvoyance agrees with the idea of the best authorities, and distinguishes between the phenomena of clairvoyance and that of telepathy, on the one hand; and between the former and that of seeing apparitions, on the other hand. I, personally, accept this distinction as both scientific in form, and as agreeing with the facts of the case. You will, of course, see that the acceptance of the existence of the astral senses throws light on many obscure points about which the psychic researchers are in doubt, and reconciles many apparently opposing facts.

All scientific authorities, as well as the best occultists, divide the phenomena of clairvoyance into several well-distinguished classes. The following classification is simple, and indicates clearly the principal forms of clairvoyant phenomena:

(1) Simple Clairvoyance, in which the clairvoyant person merely senses the auric emanations of other persons, such as the auric vibrations, colors, etc.; currents of thought-vibrations, etc.; but does not see events or scenes removed in space or time from the observer.

(2) Clairvoyance in Space, in which the clairvoyant person senses scenes and events removed in space from the observer; and, often also is able to sense such things even when they are concealed or obscured by intervening material objects.

(3) Clairvoyance in Time, in which the clairvoyant person senses scenes and events which have had their original place in past time; or scenes and events which will have their original place in the future.

I shall describe each of these three classes, with their many variations, as we reach them in their proper places in these lessons. Before doing so however, I wish to explain to you the several methods by which clairvoyant vision is usually induced. These methods may be designated as follows:

(1) Psychometry, or the method of getting en rapport with the astral plane by means of some physical object connected with the person, thing, or scene about which you desire to be informed.

(2) Crystal Gazing, etc., or the method of getting en rapport with the astral plane by means of gazing into a crystal, magic mirror, etc.

(3) Clairvoyant Reverie, or the method of getting en rapport with the astral plane by means of psychic states in which the sights, sounds and thoughts of the material and physical plane are shut out of consciousness.

I shall now proceed to give the details regarding each one of these three great classes of methods inducing clairvoyant vision, or en rapport conditions with the astral plane.

Psychometry. Psychometry is that form of clairvoyant phenomena in which the clairvoyant gets into en rapport relation with the astral plane by means of the connecting link of material objects, such as bit of stone, piece of hair, article of wearing apparel etc., which has had previous associations with the thing, person or scene regarding which clairvoyant vision is required.

Without going into technical occult explanations, I would say that the virtue of these articles consists entirely of their associative value. That is to say, they carry in them certain vibrations of past experience which serve as a connecting link, or associated filament, with the thing which is sought to be brought into the field of clairvoyant vision.

To reach clairvoyantly a thing, scene, or person in this way is akin to the unwinding of a ball of yarn, when you hold the loose end in your hand. Or, it is like giving a keen-scented dog a sniff at a handkerchief once carried by the person whom you wish him to nose out for you.

A well-known authority on the subject of psychic phenomena has said on this point: "The untrained clairvoyant usually cannot find any particular astral picture when it is wanted, without some special link to put him en rapport with the subject required. Psychometry is an instance in point. It seems as though there were a sort of magnetic attachment or affinity between any particle of matter and the record which contains its history—an affinity which enables it to act as a kind of conductor between that record and the faculties of anyone who can read it. For instance, I once brought from Stonehenge a tiny fragment of stone, not larger than a pin's head, and on putting this into an envelope and handing it to a psychometer who had no idea what it was, she at once began to describe that wonderful ruin and the desolate country surrounding it, and then went on to picture vividly what were evidently scenes from its early history, showing that the infinitessimal fragment had been sufficient to put her into communication with the records connected with the spot from which it came. The scenes through which we pass in the course of our life seem to act in the same way upon the cells of our brain as did the history of Stonehenge upon that particle of stone. They establish a connection with those cells by means of which our mind is put en rapport with that particular portion of the records, and so we 'remember' what we have seen."

One of the simplest and most common form of psychometry is that in which the psychometrist is able to tell the physical condition of a person by means of holding to the forehead, or even in the hand, some trinket or small article such as a handkerchief recently worn on the person of the individual regarding whom the information is sought. In the case of some very sensitive psychometrists, the psychic person "takes on" the condition of the other person whose former article of clothing, trinket, etc., she is holding. She will often actually experience the physical pain and distress of the person, and will be able to indicate from what ailment the person is suffering. Some persons attain great proficiency in this direction, and are a great assistance to wise physicians who avail themselves of their services. Some successful physicians themselves possess this faculty well developed, and use it to great advantage, though, as a rule they keep very quiet about it, from fear of creating unfavorable comment from their fellow-physicians and from the general public who "do not believe in such tom-foolery."

A step further is the power of some psychometrists to correctly describe the personal characteristics, and even the past history of persons with whom they come in contact, or whose "associated article" they have in their hands. Some very remarkable instances of this phase of psychometry are related in the books containing the history of clairvoyance. An interesting case is that related by Zschokke, the eminent German writer, who relates in his autobiography his wonderful experience in this direction. Listen to the story in his own words: "It has happened to me occasionally at the first meeting with a total stranger, when I have been listening in silence to his conversation, that his past life up to the present moment, with many minute circumstances belonging to one or other particular scene in it, has come across me like a dream, but distinctly, entirely involuntarily and unsought, occupying in duration a few minutes. For a long time I was disposed to consider these fleeting visions as a trick of the fancy—the more so as my dream-vision displayed to me the dress and movements of the actors, the appearance of the room, the furniture, and other accidents of the scene; till on one occasion, in a gamesome mood, I narrated to my family the secret history of a seamstress who had just quitted the room. I had never seen the person before. Nevertheless, the hearers were astonished, and laughed and would not be persuaded but that I had a previous acquaintance with the former life of the person, inasmuch as what I had stated was perfectly true.

"I was not less astonished to find that my dream vision agreed with reality. I then gave more attention to the subject, and as often as propriety allowed of it, I related to those whose lives had so passed before me the substance of my dream-vision, to obtain from them its contradiction or confirmation. On every occasion its confirmation followed, not without amazement on the part of those who gave it. On a certain fair-day I went into the town of Waldshut accompanied by two young foresters, who are still alive. It was evening, and, tired with our walk, we went into an inn called the 'Vine.' We took our supper with a numerous company at the public table, when it happened that they made themselves merry over the peculiarities of the Swiss in connection with the belief in mesmerism, Lavater's physiognomical system, and the like. One of my companions, whose national pride was touched by their raillery, begged me to make some reply, particularly in answer to a young man of superior appearance who sat opposite, and had indulged in unrestrained ridicule.

"It happened that the events of this person's life had just previously passed before my mind. I turned to him with the question whether he would reply to me with truth and candor, if I narrated to him the most secret passages of his history, he being as little known to me as I to him. That would, I suggested, go something beyond Lavater's physiognomical skill. He promised that if I told the truth he would admit it openly. Then I narrated the events with which my dream vision had furnished me, and the table learned the history of the young tradesman's life, of his school years, his peccadilloes, and finally, of a little act of roguery committed by him on the strongbox of his employer. I described the uninhabited room with its white walls, where to the right of the brown door there had stood upon the table the small money-chest, etc. The man, much struck, admitted the correctness of each circumstance—even, which I could not expect, of the last."

The above incident is typical of this class of psychometry, and many persons have had at least flashes of this phase of the power. The only remarkable thing about this particular case is its faithfulness regarding details—this shows a very fine development of the astral sense. The feature that makes it psychometric, instead of pure clairvoyance, is that the presence of the other person was necessary to produce the phenomenon—a bit of clothing would probably have answered as well. Zschokke does not seem to have been able to manifest time-clairvoyance independent of the presence of the person concerned—he needs the associated link, or loose end of the psychic ball of yarn.

Next in order in the list of the phenomena of psychometry is that in which the psychometrist is able to describe a distant scene by means of a bit of mineral, plant, or similar object, once located at that place. In such cases, the psychometrist gets en rapport with the distant scene by means of the connecting link mentioned. Having obtained this, he is able to relate the events that are happening on that scene at that particular moment. Some very interesting cases are mentioned in which the psychometrist has been able to "spy" in on a certain place, by means of some small article which has recently been located in that place. For instance I once gave a young psychometrist a penholder from the office of a lawyer, a friend of mine, located about eight hundred miles from the psychometrist. She gave a perfect picture of the interior of the office, the scene across the street visible from the office window, and certain events that were happening in the office at that moment, which were verified by careful inquiry as to persons and time. Every occultist, or investigator of psychic phenomena has experienced many cases of this kind.

Another phase of psychometry is that in which the psychometer is able to sense the conditions existing underground, by means of a piece of mineral or metal which originally was located there. Some wonderful instances of phychometric discernment of mines, etc., have been recorded. In this phase of psychometry, all that is needed is a piece of the coal, mineral or metal which has come from the mine. Following up this psychic "lead" the psychometrist is able to describe the veins or strata of the surrounding land, although they have not yet been uncovered or discovered.

Still another form of psychometric discernment is that in which the psychometrist gets en rapport with the past history of an object, or of its surroundings, by means of the object itself. In this way, the psychometrist holding in his hand, or pressing to his head, a bullet from a battle field, is able to picture the battle itself. Or, given a piece of ancient pottery or stone implement, the psychometrist is able to picture the time and peoples connected with the object in the past—sometimes after many centuries are past. I once handed a good psychometrist a bit of ornament taken from an Egyptian mummy over three thousand years old. Though the psychometrist did not know what the object was, or from whence it had come, she was able to picture not only the scenes in which the Egyptian had lived, but also the scenes connected with the manufacture of the ornament, some three hundred years before that time—for it turned out that the ornament itself was an antique when the Egyptian had acquired it. In another case, I had the psychometrist describe in detail the animal life, and the physical phenomena, of the age in which a fossil had existed when alive—many thousands of years ago. In the proper place in this book, I will explain just how it is possible to penetrate the secrets of the past by psychometric vision—that is to say, the psychic laws making the same possible.

Some of the most remarkable of recorded instances of this form of psychometry known to the Western world are those related in the works of a geologist named Denton, who some fifty years ago conducted a series of investigations into the phenomena of psychometry. His recorded experiments fill several volumes. Being a geologist, he was able to select the best subjects for the experiments, and also to verify and decide upon the accuracy of the reports given by the psychometrists. His wife, herself, was a gifted psychometrist, and it has been said of her, by good authority, that "she is able, by putting a piece of matter (whatever be its nature) to her head, to see, either with her eyes closed or open, all that the piece of matter, figuratively speaking, ever saw, heard, or experienced." The following examples will give a good idea of the Denton experiments, which are typical of this class of psychometry.

Dr. Denton gave the psychometrist a small fragment broken from a large meteorite. She held it to her head, and reported: "This is curious. There is nothing at all to be seen. I feel as if I were in the air. No, not in the air either, but in nothing, no place. I am utterly unable to describe it; it seems high, however I feel as though I were rising, and my eyes are carried upwards; but I look around in vain; there is nothing to be seen. I see clouds, now, but nothing else. They are so close to me that I seem to be in them. My head, and neck and eyes are affected. My eyes are carried up, and I cannot roll them down. Now the clouds appear lighter and lighter, and look as though the sunlight would burst through them. As the clouds separate, I can see a star or two, and then the moon instead of the sun. The moon seems near, and looks coarse and rough, and paler and larger in size than I ever saw it before. What a strange feeling comes over me! It appears as if I were going right to the moon, and it looks as if the moon were coming to me. It affects me terribly."

Dr. Denton adds: "She was too much affected to continue the experiment longer. Had this aerolite at some period of its history, come within the sphere of the moon's attraction, and had its velocity so increased that its augmented centrifugal force had carried it off into space again, whence, drawn by the superior attractive force of the earth, it had fallen and ended its career forever?"

At another time, Dr. Denton tested the psychometrist with a whalebone walking cane. She supposed it to be wood, but when she began to report her psychic impressions, they came as follows: "I feel as though I were a monster. There is nothing of a tree about it, and it is useless for me to go further. I feel like vomiting. Now I want to plunge into the water. I believe that I am going to have a fit. My jaws are large enough to take down a house at a gulp. I now know what this is—it is whalebone. I see the inside of the whale's mouth. It has no teeth. It has a slimy look, but I only get a glimpse of it. Now, I see the whole animal. What an awful looking creature."

Another time, Dr. Denton gave the psychometrist a minute piece of the enamel of the tooth of a mastodon, which had been found thirty feet below the surface of the earth. The psychometrist had not the slightest knowledge of the character of the tiny flake of enamel handed her, but nevertheless reported: "My impression is that it is a part of some monstrous animal, probably part of a tooth. I feel like a perfect monster, with heavy legs, unwieldy head, and very large body. I go down to a shallow stream to drink. I can hardly speak, my jaws are so heavy. I feel like getting down on all fours. What a noise comes through the woods. I have an impulse to answer it. My ears are very large and leathery, and I can almost fancy they flap in my face as I move my head. There are some older ones than I. It seems so out of keeping to be talking with these heavy jaws. They are dark brown, as if they had been completely tanned. There is one old fellow, with large tusks, that looks very tough. I see several younger ones. In fact, there is a whole herd. My upper lip moves curiously; I can flap it up. It seems strange to me how it is done. There is a plant growing here, higher than my head. It is nearly as thick as my wrist, very juicy, sweet, and tender—something like green corn in taste, but sweeter. It is not the taste it would have to a human being—oh no! it is sickenish, and very unpleasant to the human taste."

These instances might be multiplied indefinitely, but the principle is the same in each. In my own experience, I gave a small piece from the Great Pyramid of Egypt to a psychometrist who was uneducated and who knew nothing of ancient Egypt or its history. Notwithstanding this, she gave me such a detailed and complete account of the life of ancient Egypt, which was in such complete accordance with the opinions of the best authorities, that I would hesitate about publishing the report, for it certainly would be regarded as rank imposture by the average scientific authority. Some day, however, I may publish this.

There are no special directions to be given the student in psychometry. All that can be done is to suggest that each person should try the experiments for himself, in order to find out whether he has, or has not, the psychometric faculty. It may be developed by the methods that will be given to develop all psychic powers, in another part of this book. But much will depend upon actual practice and exercise. Take strange objects, and, sitting in a quiet room with the object held to your forehead, shut out all thoughts of the outside world, and forget all personal affairs. In a short time, if the conditions are all right, you will begin to have flashes of scenes connected with the history of the object. At first rather disconnected and more or less confused, there will soon come to you a clearing away of the scene, and the pictures will become quite plain. Practice will develop the power. Practice only when alone, or when in the presence of some sympathetic friend or friends. Always avoid discordant and inharmonious company when practicing psychic powers. The best psychometrists usually keep the physical eyes closed when practicing their power.

You have doubtless heard the sensing of sealed letters spoken of as clairvoyance. But this is merely one form of psychometry. The letter is a very good connecting medium in psychometric experiments. I advise you to begin your experiments with old letters. You will be surprised to discover how readily you will begin to receive psychic impressions from the letters, either from the person who wrote them, or from the place in which they were written, or from some one connected with the subsequent history. One of the most interesting experiments I ever witnessed in psychometry, was a case in which a letter that had been forwarded from place to place, until it had gone completely around the globe, was psychometrized by a young Hindu maiden. Although ignorant of the outside world, she was able to picture the people and scenery of every part of the globe in which the letter had traveled. Her report was really an interesting "travelogue" of a trip around the world, given in tabloid form. You may obtain some interesting results in psychometrizing old letters—but always be conscientious about it, and refrain from divulging the secrets that will become yours in the course of these experiments. Be honorable on the astral plane, as well as on the physical—more so, rather than less.

LESSON - VII

CLAIRVOYANT CRYSTAL GAZING

As I have informed you in the preceding lesson, Crystal Gazing is the second method of getting en rapport with the astral plane. Under the general term "Crystal Gazing" I include the entire body of phenomena connected with the use of the crystal, magic mirror, etc., the underlying principle being the same in all of such cases.

The crystal, etc., serves to focus the psychic energy of the person, in such a way that the astral senses are induced to function more readily than ordinarily. The student is cautioned against regarding the crystal, or magic mirror, as possessing any particular magic power in itself. On the contrary, the crystal, or magic mirror serves merely as a physical instrument for the astral vision, just as the telescope or microscope performs a similar office for the physical vision. Some persons are superstitious regarding the crystal, and accord to it some weird supernatural power, but the true occultist, understanding the laws of the phenomena arising from its use, does not fall into this error.

But, notwithstanding what I have just said, I would be neglecting my full duty in the matter if I failed to call your attention to the fact that the continued use of a particular crystal often has the effect of polarizing its molecules so as to render it a far more efficient instrument as time passes by. The longer the crystal is used by one person, the better does it seem to serve the uses of that person. I agree with many users of the crystal in their belief that each person should keep his crystal for his own personal use, and not allow it to be used indiscriminately by strangers or persons not in sympathy with occult thought. The crystal tends to become polarized according to the requirements of the person habitually using it, and it is foolish to allow this to be interfered with.

The use of crystals and other bright, shining objects, has been common to psychic investigators of all times, and in practically all lands. In the earlier days of the race, pieces of clear quartz or shining pebbles were generally employed. Sometimes pieces of polished metal were so used. In fact, nearly every object capable of being polished has been employed in this way at some time, by some person. In our own day, the same condition exists. In Australia the native sooth-sayers and magicians employ water and other shining objects, and, in some cases, even bright flame, sparks, or glowing embers. In New Zealand, the natives frequently employ drops of blood held in the hollow of the hand. The Fijians fill a hole with water, and gaze into it. South American tribes use the polished surface of black, or dark colored stones. The American Indians use water, or shining pieces or flint or quartz. Shining pieces of metal are frequently used by the primitive races. Lang, writing on the subject, has said: "They stare into a crystal ball; a cup; a mirror; a blot of ink (Egypt and India); a drop of blood (the Maoris of New Zealand); a bowl of water (American Indians); a pond (Roman and African); water in a glass bowl (Fez); or almost any polished surface, etc."

In the present-day revival of interest in crystal-gazing among the wealthier classes of Europe and America, some of the high-priced teachers have insisted upon their pupils purchasing pure crystal globes, claiming that these alone are capable of serving the purpose fully. But, as such crystals are very expensive, this advice has prevented many from experimenting. But, the advice is erroneous, for any globe of clear quartz, or even moulded glass, will serve the purpose equally well, and there is no need of spending twenty-five to fifty dollars for a pure crystal globe.

For that matter, you may obtain very good results from the use of a watch-crystal laid over a piece of black velvet. Some, today, use with the best effect small polished pieces of silver or other bright metal. Others follow the old plan of using a large drop of ink, poured into a small butter plate. Some have small cups painted black on the inside, into which they pour water—and obtain excellent results therefrom.

Above all, I caution the student to pay no attention to instructions regarding the necessity of performing incantations or ceremonies over the crystal or other object employed in crystal-gazing. This is but a bit of idle superstition, and serves no useful purpose except, possibly, that of giving the person confidence in the thing. All ceremonies of this kind have for their purpose merely the holding of the attention of the person investigating, and giving him confidence in-the result—the latter having a decided psychological value, of course.

There are but few general directions necessary for the person wishing to experiment in crystal gazing. The principal thing is to maintain quiet, and an earnest, serious state of mind—do not make a merry game of it, if you wish to obtain results. Again, always have the light behind your back, instead of facing you. Gaze calmly at the crystal, but do not strain your eyes. Do not try to avoid winking your eyes—there is a difference between "gazing" and "staring," remember. Some good authorities advise making funnels of the hands, and using them as you would a pair of opera glasses.

In many cases, a number of trials are required before you will be able to get good results. In others, at least some results are obtained at the first trial. It is a good plan to try to bring into vision something that you have already seen with the physical eyes—some familiar object. The first sign of actual psychic seeing in the crystal usually appears as a cloudy appearance, or "milky-mist," the crystal gradually losing its transparency. In this milky cloud then gradually appears a form, or face, or scene of some kind, more or less plainly defined. If you have ever developed a photographic film or plate, you will know how the picture gradually comes into view.

W.T. Stead, the eminent English investigator of psychic phenomena, has written as follows regarding the phenomena of crystal-gazing: "There are some persons who cannot look into an ordinary globular bottle without seeing pictures form themselves without any effort or will on their part, in the crystal globe. Crystal-gazing seems to be the least dangerous and most simple of all forms of experimenting. You simply look into a crystal globe the size of a five-shilling piece, or a water-bottle which is full of clear water, and which is placed so that too much light does not fall upon it, and then simply look at it. You make no incantations, and engage in no mumbo-jumbo business; you simply look at it for two or three minutes, taking care not to tire yourself, winking as much as you please, but fixing your thought upon whatever you wish to see. Then, if you have the faculty, the glass will cloud over with a milky mist, and in the centre the image is gradually precipitated in just the same way as a photograph forms on the sensitive plate."

The same authority relates the following interesting experiment with the crystal: "Miss X., upon looking into the crystal on two occasions as a test, to see if she could see me when she was several miles off, saw not me, but a different friend of mine on each occasion. She had never seen either of my friends before, but immediately identified them both on seeing them afterward at my office. On one of the evenings on which we experimented in the vain attempts to photograph a 'double,' I dined with Madam C. and her friend at a neighboring restaurant. As she glanced at the water-bottle, Madam C. saw a picture beginning to form, and, looking at it from curiosity, described with considerable detail an elderly gentleman whom she had never seen before, and whom I did not in the least recognize from her description at the moment. Three hours afterward, when the seance was over, Madam C., entered the room and recognized Mr. Elliott, of Messrs. Elliott & Fry, as the gentleman whom she had seen and described in the water-bottle at the restaurant. On another occasion the picture was less agreeable; it was an old man lying dead in bed with some one weeping at his feet; but who it was, or what it related to, no one knew."

Andrew Lang, another prominent investigator of psychic phenomena, gives the following interesting experiment in crystal-gazing: "I had given a glass ball to a young lady, Miss Baillie, who had scarcely any success with it. She lent it to Miss Leslie, who saw a large, square, old-fashioned red sofa covered with muslin (which she, afterward found in the next country-house she visited). Miss Baillie's brother, a young athlete, laughed at these experiments, took the ball into his study, and came back looking 'gey gash.' He admitted that he had seen a vision—somebody he knew, under a lamp. He said that he would discover during the week whether or not he had seen right. This was at 5:30 on a Sunday afternoon. On Tuesday, Mr. Baillie was at a dance in a town forty miles from his home, and met a Miss Preston. 'On Sunday,' he said, 'about half-past-five, you were sitting under a standard lamp, in a dress I never saw you wear, a blue blouse with lace over the shoulders, pouring out tea for a man in blue serge, whose back was toward me, so that I only saw the tip of his mustache.' 'Why, the blinds must have been up,' said Miss Preston. 'I was at Dulby,' said Mr. Baillie, and he undeniably was."

Miss X., the well-known contributor to the English magazine, "Borderland," several years ago, made a somewhat extended inquiry into the phenomena of crystal-gazing. From her experiments, she made the following classification of the phenomena of crystal-vision, which I herewith reproduce for your benefit. Her classification is as follows:

1. Images of something unconsciously observed. New reproductions, voluntary or spontaneous, and bringing no fresh knowledge to the mind.
2. Images of ideas unconsciously acquired from others. Some memory or imaginative effect, which does not come from the gazer's ordinary self. Revivals of memory. Illustrations of thought.
3. Images, clairvoyant or prophetic. Pictures giving information as to something past, present, or future, which the gazer has no other chance of knowing.

As a matter of fact, each and every form or phase of clairvoyance possible under other methods of inducing clairvoyant vision, is possible in crystal-gazing. It is a mistake to consider crystal-gazing as a separate and distinct form of psychic phenomena. Crystal-gazing is merely one particular form or method of inducing psychic or clairvoyant vision. If you will keep this in mind, you will avoid many common errors and misunderstandings in the matter.

In order to give you the benefit of as many points of view as possible, I shall now quote from an old English writer on the subject of the use of the crystal. I do this realizing that sometimes a particular student will get more from one point of view, than from another—some particular phrasing will seem to reach his understanding, where others fail. The directions of the English authority are as follows:

"What is desired through the regular use of the translucent sphere is to cultivate a personal degree of clairvoyant power, so that visions of things or events, past, present, and future, may appear clearly to the interior vision, or eye of the soul. In the pursuit of this effort only, the crystal becomes at once both a beautiful, interesting and harmless channel of pleasure and instruction, shorn of dangers, and rendered conducive to mental development.

"To the attainment of this desirable end, attention is asked to the following practical directions, which, if carefully followed, will lead to success:

"(1) Select a quiet room where you will be entirely undisturbed, taking care that it is as far as possible free from mirrors, ornaments, pictures, glaring colors, and the like, which may otherwise district the attention. The room should be of comfortable temperature, in accordance with the time of year, neither hot nor cold. About 60 to 65 deg. Fahr. is suitable in most cases, though allowance can be made where necessary for natural differences in the temperaments of various persons. Thus thin, nervous, delicately-organized individuals, and those of lymphatic and soft, easy-going, passive types, require a slightly warmer apartment than the more positive class who are known by their dark eyes, hair and complexion, combined with prominent joints. Should a fire, or any form of artificial light be necessary, it should be well screened off, so as to prevent the light rays from being reflected in, or in any manner directly reaching the crystal. The room should not be dark, but rather shadowed, or charged with a dull light, somewhat such as prevails on a cloudy or wet day.

"(2) The crystal should be placed on its stand on a table, or it may rest on a black velvet cushion, but in either case it should be partially surrounded by a black silk or similar wrap or screen, so adjusted as to cut off any undesirable reflection. Before beginning to experiment, remember that most frequently nothing will be seen on the first occasion, and possibly not for several sittings; though some sitters, if strongly gifted with psychic powers in a state of unconscious, and sometimes conscious degree of unfoldment, may be fortunate enough to obtain good results at the very first trial. If, therefore, nothing is perceived during the first few attempts, do not despair or become impatient, or imagine that you will never see anything. There is a royal road to crystal vision, but it is open only to the combined password of Calmness, Patience, and Perseverance. If at the first attempt to ride a bicycle, failure ensues, the only way to learn is to pay attention to the necessary rules, and to persevere daily until the ability to ride comes naturally. Thus it is with the would-be seer. Persevere in accordance with these simple directions, and success will sooner or later crown your efforts.

"(3) Commence by sitting comfortably with the eyes fixed upon the crystal, not by a fierce stare, but with a steady, calm gaze, for ten minutes only, on the first occasion. In taking the time it is best to hang your watch at a distance, where, while the face is clearly visible, the ticking is rendered inaudible. When the time is up, carefully put the crystal away in its case, and keep it in a dark place, under lock and key, allowing no one but yourself to handle it. At the second sitting, which should be at the same place, in the same position, and at the same time, you may increase the length of the effort to fifteen minutes, and continue for this period during the next five or six sittings, after which the time may be gradually increased, but should in no case exceed one hour. The precise order of repetition is always to be followed until the experimenter has developed an almost automatic ability to readily obtain results, when it needs no longer to be adhered to.

"(4) Any person, or persons, admitted to the room, and allowed to remain while you sit, should (a) keep absolute silence, and (b) remain seated at a distance from you. When you have developed your latent powers, questions may, of course, be put to you by one of those present, but even then in a very gentle, or low and slow tone of voice; never suddenly, or in a forceful manner.

"(5) When you find the crystal begins to look dull or cloudy, with small pin-points of light glittering therein, like tiny stars, you may know that you are commencing to obtain that for which you seek—viz., crystalline vision. Therefore, persevere with confidence. This condition may, or may not, continue for several sittings, the crystal seeming at times to alternately appear and disappear, as in a mist. By and by this hazy appearance, in its turn, will give place quite suddenly to a blindness of the senses to all else but a blue or bluish ocean of space, against which, as if it were a background, the vision will be clearly apparent.

"(6) The crystal should not be used soon after taking a meal, and care should be taken in matters of diet to partake only of digestible foods, and to avoid alcoholic beverages. Plain and nourishing food, and outdoor exercise, with contentment of mind, or love of simplicity in living, are great aids to success. Mental anxiety, or ill-health, are not conducive to the desired end. Attention to correct, breathing is of importance.

"(7) As regards the time at which events seen will come to pass, each seer is usually impressed with regard thereto; but, as a general rule, visions appearing in the extreme background indicate time more remote, either past or future, than those perceived nearer at hand, while those appearing in the foreground, or closer to the seer, denote the present or immediate future.

"(8) Two principal classes of vision will present themselves to the sitter— (a) the Symbolic, indicated by the appearance of symbols such as a flag, boat, knife, gold, etc., and (b) Actual Scenes and Personages, in action or otherwise. Persons of a positive type of organization, the more active, excitable, yet decided type, are most likely to perceive symbolically, or allegorically; while those of a passive nature usually receive direct or literal revelations. Both classes will find it necessary to carefully cultivate truthfulness, unselfishness, gratitude for what is shown, and absolute confidence in the love, wisdom, and guidance of God Himself."

As the student proceeds with the study of these lessons, he will become acquainted with various details and methods concerned with the various phases of clairvoyance, which knowledge he may then combine with the above, the whole aiding him in the successful manifestation of the psychic phenomena of crystal-gazing, which, as I have said, is merely one phase of clairvoyance and under the same general laws and rules of manifestation. Remember that present, past and future clairvoyance all is possible to the highly developed crystal gazer.

The Astral Tube. Closely allied with the phenomena of crystal-gazing, and that of psychometry, is that which occultists know as "the astral tube," although this psychic channel may be developed in ordinary clairvoyance by means of the power of concentrated attention, etc. I shall not enter into a detailed or technical discussion of the astral tube, at this place, but I wish to give you a general and comprehensive view of it and its workings.

In case of the strong concentration of the mind, in cases of psychometry or crystal-gazing, a channel or "line of force" is set up in the astral substance which composes the basis of the astral plane. This is like the wake of a ship made on the surface of the water through which the ship has passed. Or it is like a current of magnetic force in the ether. It is caused by a polarization of the particles composing the astral substance, which manifest in a current of intense vibrations in the astral substance, which thus serve as a ready channel for the transmission of psychic force or astral energy.

The astral tube serves as a ready conductor of the vibrations, currents and waves of energy on the astral plane which carry to the astral senses of the person the perception of the things, objects and scenes far removed from him in space and time. How these things far removed in space and time are perceived by the astral seer is explained in subsequent lessons of this course. At this place we are concerned merely with the "channel" through which the currents of energy flow, and which has been called the astral tube.

As a writer well says: "Through the astral tube the astral senses actually 'sense' the sights, and often the sounds, being manifested at a distance, just as one may see distant sights through a telescope, or hear distant sounds through a telephone. The astral tube is used in a variety of forms of psychic phenomena. It is often used unconsciously, and springs into existence spontaneously, under the strong influence of a vivid emotion, desire or will. It is used by the trained psychometrist, without the use of any 'starting point,' or 'focal centre,' simply by the use of his trained, developed and concentrated will. But its most familiar and common use is in connection with some object serving as a starting point or focal centre. The starting point or focal centre, above mentioned, is generally either what is known as the 'associated object' in the class of phenomena generally known as psychometry, or else a glass or crystal ball, or similar polished surface, in what is known as crystal-gazing."

Another authority tells his readers that: "Astral sight, when it is cramped by being directed along what is practically a tube, is limited very much as physical sight would be under similar circumstances, though if possessed in perfection it will continue to show, even at that distance, the auras, and therefore all the emotions and most of the thoughts of the people under observation. * * * But, it may be said, the mere fact that he is using astral sight ought to enable him to see things from all sides at once. And so it would, if he were using that sight in a normal way upon an object which was fairly near him—within his astral reach, as it were; but at a distance of hundreds or thousands of miles the case is very different. Astral sight gives us the advantage of an additional dimension, but there is still such a thing as position in that dimension, and it is naturally a potent factor in limiting Clairvoyance and Occult Powers 82 the use of the powers on that plane. * * * The limitations resemble those of a man using a telescope on the physical plane. The experimenter, for example, has a particular field of view which cannot be enlarged or altered; he is looking at his scene from a certain direction, and he cannot suddenly turn it all around and see how it looks from the other side. If he has sufficient psychic energy to spare, he may drop altogether the telescope he is using, and manufacture an entirely new one for himself which will approach his objective somewhat differently; but this is not a course at all likely to be adopted in practice."

The student will find that, as we progress, many of these points which now seem complicated and obscure will gradually take on the aspect of simplicity and clearness. We must crawl before we can walk, in psychic research as well as in everything else.

LESSON VIII

CLAIRVOYANT REVERIE

In the preceding two chapters, I have asked you to consider the first two methods of inducing the clairvoyant phenomena, namely, Psychometry, and Crystal-Gazing, respectively. In these cases you have seen how the clairvoyant gets en rapport with the astral plane by means of physical objects, in the case of psychometric clairvoyance; or by means of a shining object, in the case of crystal gazing. Let us now consider the third method of inducing the clairvoyant condition or state, i.e., by means of what may be called Clairvoyant Reverie, in which the clairvoyant gets en rapport with the astral plane by means of psychic states in which the sights, sounds and thoughts of the material and physical plane are shut out of consciousness.

The student of the general subject of clairvoyance will soon be impressed with two facts concerning the production of clairvoyant phenomena, namely, (1) that in the majority of the recorded cases of the investigators the clairvoyant phenomena were obtained when the clairvoyant was in the state of sleep, or at least semi-sleep or drowsiness, the visioning appearing more or less like a vivid dream; and (2) that in the case of the clairvoyant voluntarily entering en rapport with the astral plane, he or she would enter into what seemed to be a kind of trance condition, in some cases an absolute unconsciousness of the outside world being manifested. The student, noting these facts, is apt to arrive at the conclusion that all clairvoyance is accompanied by the condition of sleep, or trance, and that no clairvoyant phenomena are possible unless this psychic condition is first obtained. But this is only a half-truth as we shall see in a moment.

In the first place, the student arriving at this conclusion seems to have ignored the fact that the phenomena of psychometry and crystal gazing, respectively, are as true instances of clairvoyance as are those which are manifested in the sleep or trance condition. It is true that some psychometrists produce phenomena when they are in a state of psychic quiescence, but, on the other hand, many clairvoyant psychometrists merely concentrate the attention on the object before them, and remain perfectly wide-awake and conscious on the physical plane. Likewise, the average crystal gazer remains perfectly wide-awake and conscious on the physical plane. When the student takes these facts into consideration, he begins to see that the trance condition, and similar psychic states, are simply particular methods of inducing the en rapport condition for the clairvoyant, and are not inseparably bound up with the phenomena of clairvoyance.

As the student progresses, moreover, he will see that even in the case of Clairvoyant Reverie, the third method of inducing the astral en rapport condition, the clairvoyant does not always lose consciousness. In the case of many advanced and exceptionally well-developed clairvoyants, no trance or sleep condition is induced. In such cases the clairvoyant merely "shuts out" the outside world of sights, sounds and thoughts, by an effort of trained will, and then concentrates steadily on the phenomena of the astral plane. For that matter, the skilled and advanced occultist is able to function on the astral plane by simply shifting his consciousness from one plane to another, as the typist shifts from the small letters of the keyboard to the capital letters, by a mere pressure on the shift-key of the typewriter.

The only reason that many clairvoyants manifesting along the lines of the third method, known as "clairvoyant reverie," fall into the trance or sleep condition, is that they have not as yet acquired the rare art of controlling their conscious attention at will—this is something that requires great practice. They find it easier to drop into the condition of semi-trance, or semi-sleep, than it is to deliberately shut out the outer world by an act of pure will. Moreover, you will find that in the majority of the recorded cases of the investigators, the clairvoyance was more or less spontaneous on the part of the clairvoyant person, and was not produced by an act of will. As we proceed to consider the various forms and phases of clairvoyant phenomena, in these lessons, you will notice this fact. There are but few recorded cases of voluntary clairvoyance in the books of the investigators—the skilled clairvoyants, and more particularly the advanced occultists, avoid the investigators rather than seek them; they have no desire to be reported as "typical cases" of interesting psychic phenomena—they leave that to the amateurs, and those to whom the phenomena come as a wonderful revelation akin to a miracle. This accounts for the apparent predominance of this form of clairvoyance—the secret is that the net of the investigators has caught only a certain kind of psychic fish, while the others escape attention.

All this would be of no practical importance, however, were it not for the fact that the average student is so impressed by the fact that he must learn to induce the trance condition in order to manifest clairvoyant phenomena, that he does not even think of attempting to do the work otherwise. The power of auto-suggestion operates here, as you will see by a moment's thought, and erects an obstacle to his advance along voluntary lines. More than this, this mistaken idea tends to encourage the student to cultivate the trance condition, or at least some abnormal psychic condition, by artificial means. I am positively opposed to the inducing of psychic conditions by artificial means, for I consider such practices most injurious and harmful for the person using such methods. Outside of anything else, it tends to render the person negative, psychically, instead of positive—it tends to make him or her subject to the psychic influence of others, on both the physical and astral plane, instead of retaining his or her own self-control and mastery.

The best authorities among the occultists instruct their pupils that the state of clairvoyant reverie may be safely and effectively induced by the practice of mental concentration alone. They advice positively against artificial methods. A little common sense will show that they are right in this matter. All that is needed is that the consciousness shall be focused to a point—become "one pointed" as the Hindu Yogis say. The intelligent practice of concentration accomplishes this, without the necessity of any artificial methods of development, or the induction of abnormal psychic states.

If you will stop a moment and realize how easily you concentrate your attention when you are witnessing an interesting play, or listening to a beautiful rendition of some great masterpiece of musical composition, or gazing at some miracle of art, you will see what I mean. In the cases just mentioned, while your attention is completely occupied with the interesting thing before you, so that you have almost completely shut out the outer world of sound, sight and thought, you are, nevertheless, perfectly wide awake and your consciousness is alert. The same thing is true when you are reading a very interesting book—the world is shut out from your consciousness, and you are oblivious to the sights and sounds around you. At the risk of being considered flippant, I would remind you of the common spectacle of two lovers so wrapped up in each other's company that they forget that there is a smiling world of people around them—time and space are forgotten to the two lovers—to them there is only one world, with but two persons in it. Again, how often have you fallen into what is known as a "brown study," or "day dream," in which you have been so occupied with the thoughts and fancies floating through your mind, that you forgot all else. Well, then, this will give you a common-sense idea of the state that the occultists teach may be induced in order to enter into the state of en rapport with the astral plane—the state in which clairvoyance is possible. Whether you are seeking clairvoyance by the method of psychometry, or by crystal gazing, or by clairvoyant reverie—this will give you the key to the state. It is a perfectly natural state—nothing abnormal about it, you will notice.

To some who may think that I am laying too much stress on the undesirability of artificial methods of inducing the clairvoyant condition, I would say that they are probably not aware of the erroneous and often harmful teachings on the subject that are being promulgated by ignorant or misinformed teachers—"a little learning is a dangerous thing," in many cases. It may surprise some of my students to learn that some of this class of teachers are instructing their pupils to practice methods of self-hypnosis by gazing steadily at a bright object until they fall unconscious; or by gazing "cross eyed" at the tip of the nose, or at an object held between the two eyebrows. These are familiar methods of certain schools of hypnotism, and result in producing a state of artificial hypnosis, more or less deep. Such a state is most undesirable, not only by reason of its immediate effects, but also by reason of the fact that it often results in a condition of abnormal sensitiveness to the will of others, or even to the thoughts and feelings of others, on both the astral and the physical planes of life. I emphatically warn my students against any such practices, or anything resembling them.

While I dislike to dwell on the subject, I feel that I should call the attention of my students to the fact that certain teachers seek to produce the abnormal psychic condition by means of exhausting breathing exercises, which make the person dizzy and sleepy. This is all wrong. While rhythmic breathing exercises have a certain value in psychic phenomena, and are harmless when properly practiced, nevertheless such practices as those to which I have alluded are harmful to the nervous system of the person, and also tend to induce undesirable psychic conditions. Again, some teachers have sought to have their students hold their breath for comparatively long periods of time in order to bring about abnormal psychic states. The slightest knowledge of physiology informs one that such a practice must be harmful; it causes the blood to become thick and impure, and deficient in oxygen. It certainly will produce a kind of drowsiness, for the same reason that impure air in a room will do the same thing—in both cases the blood stream is poisoned and made impure. The purpose of rational and normal breathing is to obviate just this thing—so these teachers are reversing a natural law of the body, in order to produce an abnormal psychic state. With all the energy in me, I caution you against this kind of thing.

Along the same line, I protest and warn you against the practices advised by certain teachers of "psychic development," who seek to have their pupils induce abnormal physical and psychic conditions by means of drugs, odor of certain chemicals, gases, etc. Such practices, as all true occultists know, belong to the clans of the Black Magicians, or devil worshippers, of the savage races—they have no place in true occult teachings. Common sense alone should warn persons away from such things—but it seems to fail some of them. I assert without fear of intelligent contradiction, that no true occultist ever countenances any such practices as these.

All the true teachers are vigorous in their denunciation of such false teachings and harmful practices. In this same category, I place the methods which are taught by certain persons, namely, that of inducing abnormal physical and psychic condition of giddiness and haziness by means of "whirling" around in a circle until one drops from giddiness, or until one "feels queer in the head." This is a revival of the practices of certain fanatics in Persia and India, who perform it as a religious rite until they fall into what they consider a "holy sleep," but which is nothing more than an abnormal and unhealthful physical and psychic condition. Such practices are a downward step, not an upward one. It seems a pity that the necessity has arisen for such warnings as these—but my duty, as I see it, is very plain. To all who are tempted to "develop" in this way, I say, positively, "DON'T!"

The scientific, rational way to develop the astral senses is to first acquire the art of concentrating. Bear in mind that in concentration the person, while shutting out the impressions of the outside world in general, nevertheless focuses and concentrates his attention upon the one matter before him. This is quite a different thing from making oneself sensitive to every current of thought and feeling that may be in the psychic atmosphere. True concentration renders one positive, while the other methods render one negative. Contrary to the common opinion, psychic concentration is a positive state, not a negative—an active state, not a passive one. The person who is able to concentrate strongly is a master, while one who opens himself to "control," either physical or astral, is more or less of a slave to other minds.

The student who will begin by experimenting along the lines of contact mind-reading, and who then advances along the lines of true telepathy, as explained in the earlier chapters of this book, will have made a good start, and considerable progress, along the road to clairvoyant development. The rest will be largely a matter of exercise and practice. He will be aided by practicing concentration along the general lines of the best occult teaching. Such practice may consist of concentration upon almost any physical object, keeping the thing well before the mind and attention. Do not tire the attention by practicing too long at one time. The following general rules will help you in developing concentration:

(1) The attention attaches more readily to interesting rather than uninteresting things. Therefore, select some interesting thing to study and analyze by concentrated thought.

(2) The attention will decline in strength unless there is a variation in the stimulus. Therefore, keep up the power of concentration by either changing the object you are observing; or else by discovering some new properties, qualities or attributes in it.

(3) The things you wish to shut out of consciousness can best be shut out by your concentration upon some other thing—the attention can dwell only upon one thing at a time, if focused upon that one thing.

(4) The power of applying your attention, steady and undissipated, to a single object, is a mark of strong will and superior mental discipline—weak-minds cannot do this. Therefore, in cultivating concentrated attention you are really strengthening your mind and will.

(5) To develop concentrated attention, you must learn to analyze, analyze, and analyze the thing upon which you are bestowing concentrated attention. Therefore, proceed by selecting an object and analyzing it by concentrated attention, taking one part after another, one by one, until you have analyzed and mastered the whole object. Give it the same attention that the lover gives his loved one; the musician his favorite composition; the artist his favorite work of art; and the booklover his favorite book—when you have accomplished this, you have mastered concentration, and will be able to apply the mind "one pointed" upon anything you wish, physical or astral; and, consequently will have no trouble in shutting-out disturbing impressions.

(6) Learn to concentrate on the physical plane, and you will be able to concentrate on the astral plane as well. By the one who has mastered concentration, trances and abnormal psychic states will not be needed. The needle-pointed mind is able to pierce the astral veil at will, while the blunt-pointed mind is resisted and defeated by the astral envelope, which while thin is very tough and unyielding.

A well-known authority on psychic development has well said: "Occasional flashes of clairvoyance sometimes come to the highly cultured and spiritual-minded man, even though he may never have heard of the possibility of training such a faculty. In his case such glimpses usually signify that he is approaching that stage in his evolution when these powers will naturally begin to manifest themselves. Their appearance should serve as an additional stimulus to him to strive to maintain that high standard of moral purity and mental balance without which clairvoyance is a curse and not a blessing to its possessor. Between those who are entirely unimpressionable and those who are in full possession of clairvoyant power, there are many intermediate stages. Students often ask how this clairvoyant faculty will first be manifested in themselves—how they may know when they have reached the stage at which its first faint foreshadowings are beginning to be visible. Cases differ so widely that it is impossible to give to this question any answer that will be universally applicable.

"Some people begin by a plunge, as it were, and under some unusual stimulus become able just for once to see some striking vision; and very often in such a case, because the experience does not repeat itself, the seer comes in time to believe that on that occasion he must have been the victim of hallucination. Others begin by becoming intermittently conscious of the brilliant colors and vibrations of the human aura; yet others find themselves with increasing frequency seeing and hearing something to which those around them are blind and deaf; others, again, see faces, landscapes, or colored clouds floating before their eyes in the dark before they sink to rest; while perhaps the commonest experience of all is that of those who begin to recollect with greater and greater clearness what they have seen and heard on other planes during sleep."

The authority in question gives the following excellent advice regarding the subject of the development of clairvoyant power and astral visioning: "Now the fact is that there are many methods by which it may be developed, but only one which can be at all safely recommended for general use—that of which we shall speak last of all. Among the less advanced nations of the world the clairvoyant state has been produced in various objectionable ways; among some of the non-Aryan tribes of India, by the use of intoxicating drugs or the inhaling of stupefying fumes; among the dervishes, by whirling in a mad dance of religious fervor until vertigo and insensibility supervene; among the followers of the abominable practices of the Voodoo cult, by frightful sacrifices and loathsome rites of black magic. Methods such as these are happily not in vogue in our own race, yet even among us large numbers of dabblers in this ancient art adopt some plan of self-hypnotization, such as gazing at a bright spot, or the repetition of some formula until a condition of semi-stupefaction is produced; while yet another school among them would endeavor to arrive at similar results by the use of some of the Indian systems of regulation of the breath. All these methods are unequivocally to be condemned as quite unsafe for the practice of the ordinary man who has no idea of what he is doing—who is simply making vague experiments in an unknown world. Even the method of obtaining clairvoyance by allowing oneself to be mesmerized by another person is one from which I should myself shrink with the most decided distaste; and assuredly it should never be attempted except under conditions of absolute trust and affection between the magnetizer and the magnetized, and a perfection of purity in heart and soul, in mind and intention, such as is rarely to be seen among any but the greatest of saints.

"Yet there is one practice which is advised by all religions alike—which if adopted carefully and reverently can do no harm to any human being, yet from which a very pure type of clairvoyance has sometimes been developed; and that is the practice of meditation. Let a man choose a certain time every day—a time when he can rely upon being quiet and undisturbed, though preferably in the daytime rather than at night—and set himself at that time to keep his mind for a few minutes entirely free from all earthly thoughts of any kind whatever, and, when that is achieved, to direct the whole force of his being towards the highest ideal that he happens to know. He will find that to gain such perfect control of thought is enormously more difficult than he supposes, but when he attains it it cannot but be in every way most beneficial to him, and as he grows more and more able to elevate and concentrate his thought, he may gradually find that new worlds are opening before his sight. As a preliminary training towards the satisfactory achievement of such meditation, he will find it desirable to make a practice of concentration in the affairs of daily life—even in the smallest of them. If he writes a letter, let him think of nothing else but that letter until it is finished; if he reads a book, let him see to it that his thought is never allowed to wander from his author's meaning. He must learn to hold his mind in check, and to be master of that also, as well as of his lower passions; he must patiently labor to acquire absolute control of his thoughts, so that he will always know exactly what he is thinking about, and why—so that he can use his mind, and turn it or hold it still, as a practiced swordsman turns his weapon where he will."

I have given the above full quotation from this authority, not merely because that from another angle he states the same general principles as do I; but also because his personal experience in actual clairvoyant phenomena is so extended and varied that any word from him on the subject of the development of clairvoyant power must have a value of its own. While I differ from this authority on some points of detail of theory and practice, nevertheless I gladly testify to the soundness of his views as above quoted, and pass them on to my students for careful consideration and attention. The student will do well to heed what he has to say, and to combine such opinion with what I have uttered in the earlier part of this chapter—there will be found a close agreement in principle and practice.

And, now let us pass on to a consideration of the various forms and phases of the clairvoyant phenomena itself. The subject is fascinating, and I am Clairvoyance and Occult Powers 92 sure that you will enjoy this little excursion into the strange realm of thought regarding the astral phenomena of clairvoyance. But, be sure to master each lesson before proceeding to the rest, as otherwise you will have to turn back the leaves of the course in order to pick up some point of teaching that you have neglected.

LESSON - IX

SIMPLE CLAIRVOYANCE

In a previous chapter we have seen that there are three well-defined classes of clairvoyance, namely, (1) Simple clairvoyance; (2) Clairvoyance in space; and (3) Clairvoyance in Time. I shall now consider these in sequence, beginning with the first, Simple Clairvoyance.

In simple clairvoyance the clairvoyant person merely senses the auric emanations of other persons, such as the auric vibrations, colors, etc., currents of thought vibrations, etc., but does not see events or scenes removed in space or time from the observer. There are other phenomena peculiar to this class of clairvoyance which I shall note as we progress with this chapter.

An authority on the subject of astral phenomena has written interestingly, as follows, regarding some of the phases of simple clairvoyance: "When we come to consider the additional facilities which it offers in the observation of animate objects, we see still more clearly the advantages of astral vision. It exhibits to the clairvoyant the aura of plants and animals, and thus in the case of the latter their desires and emotions, and whatever thoughts they may have, are all plainly shown before his eyes. But it is in dealing with human beings that he will most appreciate the value of this faculty, for he will often be able to help them far more effectually when he guides himself by the information which it gives him.

"He will be able to see the aura as far up as the astral body, and though that leaves all the higher part of a man still hidden from his gaze, he will nevertheless find it possible by careful observation to learn a good deal about the higher part from what is within his reach. His capacity of examination of the etheric double will give him considerable advantage in locating and classifying any defects or diseases of the nervous system, while from the appearance of the astral body he will at once be aware of all the emotions, passions, desires and tendencies of the man before him, and even of very many of his thoughts also.

"As he looks at a person he will see him surrounded by the luminous mist of the astral aura, flashing with all sorts of brilliant colors, and constantly changing in hue and brilliancy with every variation of the person's thoughts and feelings. He will see this aura flooded with the beautiful rose-color of pure affection, the rich blue of devotional feeling, the hard, dull brown of selfishness, the deep scarlet of anger, the horrible lurid red of sensuality, the livid grey of fear, the black clouds of hatred and malice, or any of the other hundredfold indications so easily to be read in it by the practiced eye; and thus it will be impossible for any persons to conceal from him the real state of their feelings on any subject. Not only does the astral aura show him the temporary result of the emotion passing through it at the moment, but it also gives him, by an arrangement and proportion of its colors when in a condition of comparative rest, a clue to the general disposition and character of its owner."

By simple clairvoyance in a certain stage of development the clairvoyant person is able to sense the presence of the human aura, by means of his astral sight. The human aura, as all students of occultism know, is that peculiar emanation of astral vibrations that extends from each living human being, surrounding him in an egg-shaped form for a distance of two to three feet on all sides. This peculiar nebulous envelope is not visible to the physical sight, and may be discerned only by means of the astral senses. It, however, may be dimly "felt" by many persons coming into the presence of other persons, and constitutes a personal atmosphere which is sensed by other persons.

The trained clairvoyant vision sees the human aura as a nebulous hazy substance, like a luminous cloud, surrounding the person for two or three feet on each side of his body, being more dense near the body and gradually becoming less dense as it extends away from the body. It has a phosphorescent appearance, with a peculiar tremulous motion manifesting through its substance. The clairvoyant sees the human aura as composed of all the colors of the spectrum, the combination shifting with the changing mental and emotional states of the person. But, in a general way, it may be said that each person has his or her or distinctive astral auric colors, depending upon his or her general character or personality. Each mental state, or emotional manifestation, has its own particular shade or combination of shades of auric coloring. This beautiful kaleidoscopic spectacle has its own meaning to the advanced occultist with clairvoyant vision, for he is able to read the character and general mental states of the person by means of studying his astral auric colors. I have explained these auric colors, and their meanings, in my little book entitled "The Human Aura."

The human aura is not always in a state of calm phosphorescence, however. On the contrary, it sometimes manifests great flames, like those of a fiery furnace, which shoot forth in great tongues, and dart forth suddenly in certain directions toward the objects attracting them. Under great emotional excitement the auric flames move around in swift circling whirlpools, or else swirl away from a centre. Again, it seems to throw forth tiny glistening sparks of astral vibrations, some of which travel for great distance.

The clairvoyant vision is also able to discern what is called the "prana aura" of a person. By this term is indicated that peculiar emanation of vital force which surrounds the physical body of each and every person. In fact, many persons of but slight clairvoyant power, who cannot sense the auric colors, are able to perceive this prana-aura without trouble. It is sometimes called the "health aura," or "physical aura." It is colorless, or rather about the shade of clear glass, diamond, or water. It is streaked with very minute, bristle-like lines. In a state of good health, these fine lines are stiff like toothbrush bristles; while, in cases of poor health, these lines droop, curl and present a furlike appearance. It is sometimes filled with minute sparkling particles, like tiny electric sparks in rapid vibratory motion.

To the clairvoyant vision the prana-aura appears like the vibrating heated air arising from a fire, or stove, or from the heated earth in summer. If the student will close his eyes partially, and will peer through narrowed eyelids, he will in all probability be able to perceive this prana-aura surrounding the body of some healthy, vigorous person—particularly if the person is sitting in a dim light. Looking closely, he will see the peculiar vibratory motion, like heated air, at a distance of about two inches from the body of the person. It requires a little practice in order to acquire the knack of perceiving these vibrations—a little experimenting in order to get just the right light on the person—but practice will bring success, and you will be repaid for your trouble.

In the same way, the student may by practice acquire the faculty to perceiving his own prana-aura. The simplest way to obtain this last mentioned result is to place your fingers (spread out in fan-shape) against a black background, in a dim light. Then gaze at the fingers with narrowed eyelids, and half-closed eyes. After a little practice, you will see a fine thin line surrounding your fingers on all sides—a semi-luminous border of prana-aura. In most cases this border of aura is colorless, but sometimes a very pale yellowish hue is perceived. The stronger the vital force of the person, the stronger and brighter will this border of prana-aura appear. The aura surrounding the fingers will appear very much like the semi-luminous radiance surrounding a gas-flame, or the flame of a candle, which is familiar to nearly everyone.

Another peculiar phenomenon of the astral plane, perceived by clairvoyants of a certain degree of development, is that which is known as the "thought-form." A thought-form is a specialized grouping of astral substance, crystalized by the strong thought impulses or vibrations of a person thinking, or manifesting strong emotional excitement. It is generated in the aura of the person, in the first place, but is then thrown off or emitted from the atmosphere of the person, and is sent off into space. A thought-form is really but a strongly manifested thought or feeling which has taken form in the astral substance. Its power and duration depend upon the degree of force of the thought or feeling manifesting it.

These thought-forms differ very materially from one another in form and general appearance. The most common form is that of a tiny series of waves, similar to those caused by the dropping of a pebble in a pond of water. Sometimes the thought-form takes on the appearance of a whirlpool, rotating around a centre, and moving through space as well. Another form is like that of the pin-wheel fireworks, swirling away from its centre as it moves through space. Still another form is that of a whirling ring, like that emitted from a smokestack of a locomotive, or the mouth of a smoker—the familiar "ring" of the smoker. Others have the form and appearance of semi-luminous globes, glowing like a giant opal.

Other thought-forms are emitted in jet-like streams, like steam puffed out from a tea-kettle. Again, it will appear as a series of short puffs of steam-like appearance. Again, it will twist along like an eel or snake. Another time it will twist its way like a corkscrew. At other times it will appear as a bomb, or series of bombs projected from the aura of the thinker. Sometimes, as in the case of a vigorous thinker or speaker, these thought-form bombs will be seen to explode when they reach the aura of the person addressed or thought of. Other forms appear like nebulous things resembling an octopus, whose twining tentacles twist around the person to whom they are directed.

Each thought-form bears the same color that it possessed when generated in the aura of its creator, though the colors seem to fade with time. Many of them glow with a dull phosphorescence, instead of bright coloring. The atmosphere of every person, and every place, is filled with various thought-forms emanated from the person, or persons who inhabit the place. Each building has its own distinctive thought-forms, which permeate its mental atmosphere, and which are clearly discernible by trained clairvoyant vision.

I here take the liberty of quoting a few paragraphs from my little book entitled "The Astral World," in which the phenomena of the astral plane are explained in detail. I reproduce them here in order to show you what you may see on the astral plane when your clairvoyant vision is sufficiently developed to function there. The words are addressed to one who is sensing on the astral, plane.

"Notice that beautiful spiritual blue around that woman's head! And see that ugly muddy red around that man passing her! Here comes an intellectual giant—see that beautiful golden yellow around his head, like a nimbus! But I don't exactly like that shade of red around his body—and there is too marked an absence of blue in his aura! He lacks harmonious development. Do you notice those great clouds of semi-luminous substance, which are slowly floating along?—notice how the colors vary in them. Those are clouds of thought vibrations, representing the composite thought of a multitude of people. Also notice how each body of thought is drawing to itself little fragments of similar thought-forms and energy. You see here the tendency of thought-forms to attract others of their kind—how like the proverbial birds of a feather, they flock together—how thoughts come home, bringing their friends with them—how each man creates his own thought atmosphere.

"Speaking of atmospheres, do you notice that each shop we pass has its own peculiar thought-atmosphere? If you look into the houses on either side of the street, you will see that the same thing is true. The very street itself has its own atmosphere, created by the composite thought of those inhabiting and frequenting it. No! do not pass down that side street—its astral atmosphere is too depressing, and its colors too horrible and disgusting for you to witness just now—you might get discouraged and fly back to your physical body for relief. Look at those thought-forms flying through the atmosphere! What a variety of form and coloring! Some most beautiful, the majority quite neutral in tint, and occasionally a fierce, fiery one tearing its way along toward its mark. Observe those whirling and swirling thought-forms as they are thrown off from that business-house. Across the street, notice that great octopus monster of a thought-form, with its great tentacles striving to wind around persons and draw them into that flashy dance-hall and dram-shop. A devilish monster which we would do well to destroy. Turn your concentrated thought upon it, and will it out of existence—there, that's the right way; watch it sicken and shrivel! But, alas! more of its kind will come forth from that place."

The above represents the sights common to the advanced occultist who explores the astral plane either in his astral body, or else by means of clairvoyant vision. To such a one, these sights are just as natural as those of the physical plane to the person functioning by ordinary physical senses. One is as natural as is the other—there is nothing supernatural about either.

But there are other, and even more wonderful attributes of astral visioning than that which we have just related. Let us take a general survey of these, so that you may be familiar with what you hope to see on the astral plane, and which you will see when you have sufficiently developed your clairvoyant powers.

What would you think if you could "see through a brick wall?" Well, the clairvoyant is able to do this. For that matter, the physical X Rays are able to penetrate through solid substances, and the astral vibrations are even more subtle than these. It seems strange to hear of this kind of visioning as purely natural, doesn't it? It smacks strongly of the old supernatural tales—but it is as simply natural as is the X Ray. The advanced clairvoyant is able to see through the most solid objects, and inside of anything, for that matter. The astral senses register the subtle vibrations of the astral plane, just as the physical eye registers the ordinary rays of light-energy. You are able to see through solid glass, with the physical eye, are you not? Well, in the same way the clairvoyant sees through solid steel or granite. It is all a matter of registering vibrations of energy—nothing more, and nothing less.

It is in this way that the trained clairvoyant is able to read from closed books, sealed letters, etc. In the same way, he is able to pierce the dense soil, and to see far down into the depths of the earth, subject to certain limitations. Veins of coal, oil, and other substances have been discovered clairvoyantly in this way. Not every clairvoyant is able to do this, but the advanced ones have done it. In the same way, the trained clairvoyant is able to see inside the bodies of sick persons, and to diagnose their ailments, providing, of course, he is familiar with the appearance of the organs in health and in disease, and has a sufficient knowledge of physiology and pathology to interpret what he sees.

An authority on the phenomena of the astral plane has written entertainingly and correctly regarding this phase of simple clairvoyance, as follows: "The possession of this extraordinary and scarcely expressible power, then, must always be borne in mind through all that follows. It lays every point in the interior of every solid body absolutely open to the gaze of the seer, just as every point in the interior of a circle lies open to the gaze of a man looking down upon it. But even this is by no means all that it gives to its possessor. He sees not only the inside as well as the outside of every object, but also its astral counterpart. Every atom and molecule of physical matter has its corresponding astral atoms and molecules, and the mass which is built up out of these is clearly visible to the clairvoyant. Usually the astral form of any object projects somewhat beyond the physical part of it, and thus metals, stones and other things are seen surrounded by an astral aura.

"It will be seen at once that even in the study of inorganic matter a man gains immensely by the acquisition of this vision. Not only does he see the astral part of the object at which he looks, which before was wholly hidden from him; not only does he see much more of its physical constitution than he did before, but even what was visible to him before is now seen much more clearly and truly. * * * Another strange power of which he may find himself in possession is that of magnifying at will the minutest physical or astral particle to any desired size, as through a microscope—though no microscope ever made, or ever likely to be made, possesses even a thousandth part of this psychic magnifying power. By its means the hypothetical molecule and atom postulated by science become visible and living realities to the occult student, and on this closer examination he finds them to be much more complex in their structure than the scientific man has yet realized them to be. It also enables him to follow with the closest attention and the most lively interest all kinds of electrical, magnetic, and other etheric action; and when some of the specialists in these branches of science are able to develop the power to see these things whereof they write so facilely, some very wonderful and beautiful revelations may be expected.

"This is one of the SIDDIHIS or powers described in the Oriental books as accruing to the man who devotes himself to spiritual development, though the name under which it is there mentioned might not be immediately recognizable. It is referred to as 'the power of making oneself large or small at will,' and the reason of a description which appears so oddly to reverse the fact is that in reality the method by which this feat is performed is precisely that indicated in these ancient books. It is by the use of temporary visual machinery of inconceivable minuteness that the world of the infinitely little is so clearly seen; and in the same way (or rather in the opposite way) it is by enormously increasing the size of the machinery used that it becomes possible to increase the breadth of one's view—in the physical sense as well as, let us hope, in the moral—far beyond anything that science has ever dreamt of as possible for man. So that the alteration in size is really in the vehicle of the student's consciousness, and not in anything outside of himself; and the old Oriental books have, after all, put the case more accurately than have we. I have indicated, though only in the roughest outlines, what a trained student, possessed of full astral vision, would see in the immensely wider world to which that vision introduced him; but I have said nothing of the stupendous change in his mental attitude which comes from the experimental certainty regarding matters of paramount importance. The difference between even the profoundest intellectual conviction, and the precise knowledge gained by direct personal experience, must be felt in order to be appreciated."

Now, here at this place, I wish to call the attention of the student to the fact that while the above stated, phenomena strictly belong to the class of "simple clairvoyance," rather than to "space clairvoyance," or "time clairvoyance" respectively, nevertheless the same phenomena may be manifested in connection with that of these other classes of clairvoyance. For instance, in space clairvoyance the trained clairvoyant is able not only to perceive things happening at points far distant, but may also (if highly developed psychically) be able to perceive the details just mentioned as well as if he were at that distant point in person. Likewise, in time clairvoyance, the clairvoyant may exercise the power of magnifying vision regarding the object far distant in time, just as if he were living in that time. So here as elsewhere we find the different classes of phenomena shading and blending into each other. At the best, classifications are useful principally for convenience in intellectual consideration and reasoning.

In the same way, the clairvoyant may manifest the above mentioned forms of astral sensing in cases when the astral vision has been awakened by psychometry, or by crystal gazing, as well as in those cases in which the condition has been brought about through meditation, or similar methods.

I would also call the attention of the student to the fact that in the above description of the phenomena of simple clairvoyance I have made no mention of the sights of the astral plane which often become visible to the clairvoyant, and which have to do with astral bodies, astral shells, the disembodied souls of those who have passed on to other planes of existence, etc. I shall take up these matters in other parts of this course, and shall not dwell upon them in this place. But, I wish you to remember that the same power which enables you to sense other objects by means of the astral scenes, is the same that is called into operation in the cases to which I have just referred.

The astral plane is a wonderful plane or field of being, containing many strange and wonderful beings and things. The person living on the physical plane may visit the astral plane in the astral body; and, again, he may perceive the happenings and scenes of that plane by means of the awakened and developed astral senses. Some clairvoyants find it easy to function in one way, and some in another. It is reserved for the scientifically developed clairvoyant to manifest the well-rounded power to perceive the phenomena of the astral plane in its wonderful entirety.

Finally, you will see by reference to other chapters of this book, that one may manifest simple clairvoyant powers (as well as the more complicated ones of time and space clairvoyance) not only in the ordinary waking state, but also in the state of dreams. In fact, some of the most striking psychic phenomena are manifested when the seer is in the dream state. As we proceed, you will find that every phase of the great subject will fit into its place, and will be found to blend with every other phase. There will be found a logical harmony and unity of thought pervading the whole subject. But we must use single bricks and stones as we build—it is only in the completed structure that we may perceive the harmonious unity.

LESSON - X

CLAIRVOYANCE OF DISTANT SCENES

Let us now consider the phenomena of the second class of clairvoyance, namely, Clairvoyance in Space.

In space clairvoyance the clairvoyant person senses scenes and events removed in space from the observer—that is to say, scenes and events situated outside of the range of the physical vision of the clairvoyant. In this class also is included certain phenomena in which the clairvoyant vision is able to discern things that may be concealed or obscured by intervening material objects. Some of the many different forms and phases of space clairvoyance are illustrated by the following examples, all taken from the best sources.

Bushnell relates the following well-known case of space clairvoyance: "Capt. Yount, of Napa Valley, California, one midwinter's night had a dream in which he saw what appeared to be a company of emigrants arrested by the snows of the mountains, and perishing rapidly by cold and hunger. He noted the very cast of the scenery, marked by a huge, perpendicular front of white-rock cliff; he saw the men cutting off what appeared to be tree-tops rising out of deep gulfs of snow; he distinguished the very features of the persons, and their look of peculiar distress. He awoke profoundly impressed by the distinctness and apparent reality of the dream. He at length fell asleep, and dreamed exactly the same dream over again. In the morning he could not expel it from his mind. Falling in shortly after with an old hunter comrade, he told his story, and was only the more deeply impressed by him recognizing without hesitation the scenery of the dream. This comrade came over the Sierra by the Carson Valley Pass, and declared that a spot in the Pass exactly answered his description.

"By this the unsophistical patriarch was decided. He immediately collected a company of men, with mules and blankets and all necessary provisions. The neighbors were laughing meantime at his credulity. 'No matter,' he said, 'I am able to do this, and I will, for I verily believe that the fact is according to my dream.' The men were sent into the mountains one hundred and fifty miles distant, direct to the Carson Valley Pass. And there they found the company exactly in the condition of the dream, and brought in the remnant alive."

In connection with this case, some leading, occultists are of the opinion that the thought-waves from the minds of the distressed lost persons reached Capt. Yount in his sleep, and awakened his subconscious attention. Having natural clairvoyant power, though previously unaware of it, he naturally directed his astral vision to the source of the mental currents, and perceived clairvoyantly the scene described in the story. Not having any acquaintance with any of the lost party, it was only by reason of the mental currents of distress so sent out that his attention was attracted. This is a very interesting case, because several psychic factors are involved in it, as I have just said.

In the following case, there is found a connecting link of acquaintance with a person playing a prominent part in the scene, although there was no conscious appeal to the clairvoyant, nor conscious interest on her part regarding the case. The story is well-known, and appears in the Proceedings of the Society for Psychical Research. It runs as follows:

"Mrs. Broughton awoke one night in 1844, and roused her husband, telling him that something dreadful had happened in France. He begged her to go asleep again, and not trouble him. She assured him that she was not asleep when she saw what she insisted on telling him—what she saw in fact. She saw, first, a carriage accident, or rather, the scene of such an accident which had occurred a few moments before. What she saw was the result of the accident—a broken carriage, a crowd collected, a figure gently raised and carried into the nearest house, then a figure lying on a bed, which she recognized as the Duke of Orleans. Gradually friends collected around the bed—among them several members of the French royal family—the queen, then the king, all silently, tearfully, watching the evidently dying duke. One man (she could see his back, but did not know who he was) was a doctor. He stood bending over the duke, feeling his pulse, with his watch in the other hand. And then all passed away, and she saw no more.

"As soon as it was daylight she wrote down in her journal all that she had seen. It was before the days of the telegraph, and two or more days passed before the newspapers announced 'The Death of the Duke of Orleans.' Visiting Paris a short time afterwards, she saw and recognized the place of the accident, and received the explanation of her impression. The doctor who attended the dying duke was an old friend of hers, and as he watched by the bed his mind had been constantly occupied with her and her family."

In many cases of clairvoyance of this kind, there is found to exist a strong connecting link of mutual interest or affection, over which flows the strong attention-arousing force of need or distress, which calls into operation the clairvoyant visioning.

In other cases there seems to be lacking any connecting link, although, even in such cases there may be a subconscious link connecting the clairvoyant with the scene or event. An interesting example of this last mentioned phase is that related by W.T. Stead, the English editor and author, as having happened to himself. Mr. Stead's recital follows:

"I got into bed and was not able to go to sleep. I shut my eyes and waited for sleep to come; instead of sleep, however, there came to me a succession of curiously vivid clairvoyant pictures. There was no light in the room, and it was perfectly dark; I had my eyes shut also. But, notwithstanding the darkness, I suddenly was conscious of looking at a scene of singular beauty. It was as if I saw a living miniature about the size of a magic-lantern slide. At this moment I can recall the scene as if I saw it again. It was a seaside piece. The moon was shining upon the water, which rippled slowly on to the beach. Right before me a long mole ran into the water. On either side of the mole irregular rocks stood up above the sea-level. On the shore stood several houses, square and rude, which resembled nothing that I had ever seen in house architecture. No one was stirring, but the moon was there and the sea and the gleam of the moonlight on the rippling waters, just as if I had been looking on the actual scene. It was so beautiful that I remember thinking that if it continued I should be so interested in looking at it that I should never go asleep. I was wide awake, and at the same time that I saw the scene I distinctly heard the dripping of the rain outside the window. Then, suddenly without any apparent object or reason, the scene changed.

"The moonlight sea vanished, and in us place I was looking right into the interior of a reading-room. It seemed as if it had been used as a school-room in the daytime, and was employed as a reading-room in the evening. I remember seeing one reader who had a curious resemblance to Tim Harrington, although it was not he, hold up a magazine or book in his hand and laugh. It was not a picture—it was there. The scene was just as if you were looking through an opera glass; you saw the play of the muscles, the gleaming of the eye, every movement of the unknown persons in the unnamed place into which you were gazing. I saw all that without opening my eyes, nor did my eyes have anything to do with it. You see such things as these as if it were with another sense which is more inside your head than in your eyes. The pictures were apropos of nothing; they had been suggested by nothing I had been reading or talking of; they simply came as if I had been able to look through a glass at what was occurring somewhere else in the world. I had my peep, and then it passed."

An interesting case of space clairvoyance is that related of Swedenborg, on the best authority. The story runs that in the latter part of September, 1759, at four o'clock one Saturday afternoon, Swedenborg arrived home from England, and disembarked at the town of Gothenburg. A friend, Mr. W. Castel, met him and invited him to dinner, at which meal there were fifteen persons gathered around the table in honor of the guest. At six o'clock, Swedenborg went out a few minutes, returning to the table shortly thereafter, looking pale and excited. When questioned by the guests he replied that there was a fire at Stockholm, two hundred miles distant, and that the fire was steadily spreading. He grew very restless, and frequently left the room. He said that the house of one of his friends, whose name he mentioned, was already in ashes, and that his own was in danger. At eight o'clock, after he had been out again, he returned crying out cheerfully, "Thank heaven! the fire is out, the third door from my house!" The news of the strange happening greatly excited the people of the town, and the city officials made inquiry regarding it. Swedenborg was summoned before the authorities, and requested to relate in detail what he had seen. Answering the questions put to him, he told when and how the fire started; how it had begun; how, when and where it had stopped; the time it had lasted; the number of houses destroyed or damaged, and the number of persons injured. On the following Monday morning a courier arrived from Stockholm, bringing news of the fire, having left the town while it was still burning. On the next day after, Tuesday morning, another courier arrived at the city hall with a full report of the fire, which corresponded precisely with the vision of Swedenborg. The fire had stopped precisely at eight o'clock, the very minute that Swedenborg had so announced it to the company.

A similar case is related by Stead, having been told to him by the wife of a Dean in the Episcopal Church. He relates it as follows: "I was staying in Virginia, some hundred miles away from home, when one morning about eleven o'clock I felt an overpowering sleepiness, which drowsiness was quite unusual, and which caused me to lie down. In my sleep I saw quite distinctly my home in Richmond in flames. The fire had broken out in one wing of the house, which I saw with dismay was where I kept all my best dresses. The people were all trying to check the flames, but it was no use. My husband was there, walking about before the burning house, carrying a portrait in his hand. Everything was quite clear and distinct, exactly as if I had actually been present and seen everything. After a time, I woke up, and going down stairs told my friends the strange dream I had had. They laughed at me, and made such game of my vision that I did my best to think no more about it. I was traveling about, a day or two passed, and when Sunday came I found myself in a church where some relatives were worshipping. When I entered the pew they looked very strange, and as soon as the service was over I asked them what was the matter. 'Don't be alarmed,' they said, 'there is nothing serious.' Then they handed me a post-card from my husband which simply said, 'House burned out; covered by insurance.' The day was the date upon which my dream occurred. I hastened home, and then I learned that everything had happened exactly as I had seen it. The fire had broken out in the wing I had seen blazing. My clothes were all burned, and the oddest thing about it was that my husband, having rescued a favorite picture from the burning building, had carried it about among the crowd for some time before he could find a place in which to put it safely."

Another case, related by Stead, the same authority, runs as follows: "The father of a son who had sailed on the 'Strathmore,' an emigrant ship outbound from the Clyde saw one night the ship foundering amid the waves, and saw that his son, with some others, had escaped safely to a desert island near which the wreck had taken place. He was so much impressed by this vision that he wrote to the owner of the 'Strathmore' telling him what he had seen. His information was scouted; but after a while the 'Strathmore' became overdue, and the owner became uneasy. Day followed day, and still no tidings of the missing ship. Then like Pharaoh's butler, the owner remembered his sins one day, and hunted up the letter describing the vision. It supplied at least a theory to account for the ship's disappearance. All outward-bound ships were requested to look out for any survivors on the island indicated in the vision. These orders were obeyed, and the survivors of the 'Strathmore' were found exactly where the father had seen them."

The Society for Psychical Research mentions another interesting case, as follows: "Dr. Golinski, a physician of Kremeutchug, Russia, was taking an after-dinner nap in the afternoon, about half-past three o'clock. He had a vision in which he saw himself called out on a professional visit, which took him to a little room with dark hangings. To the right of the door he saw a chest of drawers, upon which rested a little paraffine lamp of special pattern, different from anything he had ever seen before. On the left of the door, he saw a woman suffering from a severe hemorrhage. He then saw himself giving her professional treatment. Then he awoke, suddenly, and saw that it was just half-past four o'clock. Within ten minutes after he awoke, he was called out on a professional visit, and on entering the bedroom he saw all the details that had appeared to him in his vision. There was the chest of drawers—there was the peculiar lamp—there was the woman on the bed, suffering from the hemorrhage. Upon inquiry, he found that she had grown worse between three and four o'clock, and had anxiously desired that he come to her about that time, finally dispatching a messenger for him at half-past four, the moment at which he awoke."

Another, and a most peculiar, phase of space clairvoyance is that in which certain persons so awaken the astral senses of other persons that these persons perceive the first person—usually in the form of seemingly seeing the person present in the immediate vicinity, just as one would see a ghostly visitor. In some cases there is manifested double-clairvoyance, both persons visioning clairvoyantly; in other cases, only the person "visited" astrally senses the occurrence. The following cases illustrate this form of space clairvoyance.

W.T. Stead relates the case of a lady well known to him, who spontaneously developed the power of awakening astral perception in others. She seemed to "materialize" in their presence. Her power in this direction became a source of considerable anxiety and worry to her friends to whom she would pay unexpected and involuntary visits, frightening them out of their wits by the appearance of her "ghost." They naturally thought that she had died suddenly and had appeared to them in ghostly form. The lady, her self, was totally unconscious of the appearance, though she admitted that at or about the times of the appearances she had been thinking of her friends whom she visited astrally.

The German writer, Jung Stilling, mentions the case of a man of good character who had developed power of this kind, but also was conscious of his visits. He exerted the power consciously by an effort of will, it seems. At one time he was consulted by the wife of a sea captain whose husband was on a long voyage to Europe and Asia (sailing from America). His ship was long overdue, and his wife was quite worried about him. She consulted the gentleman in question, and he promised to do what he could for her. Leaving the room he threw himself on a couch and was seen by the lady (who peered through the half-opened door) to be in a state of semi-trance. Finally he returned and told her that he had visited her husband in a coffee-house in London, and gave her husband's reasons for not writing, adding that her husband would soon return to America. When her husband returned several months later, the wife asked him about the matter. He informed her that the clairvoyant's report was correct in every particular. Upon being introduced to the clairvoyant, the captain manifested great surprise, saying that he had met the man in question on a certain day in a coffee-house in London, and that the man had told him that his wife was worried about him, and that he had told the man that he had been prevented from writing for several reasons, and that he was on the eve of beginning his return voyage to America. He added that when he looked for the man a few moments afterwards, the stranger had apparently lost himself in the crowd, disappeared and was seen no more by him.

The Society for Psychical Research gives prominence to the celebrated case of the member of the London Stock Exchange, whose identity it conceals under the initials "S.H.B.," who possessed this power of voluntary awakening of astral sight in others by means of his "appearance" to them. The man relates his experience to the Society as follows: "One Sunday night in November, 1881, I was in Kildare Gardens, when I willed very strongly that I would visit in the spirit two lady friends, the Misses X., who were living three miles off, in Hogarth Road. I willed that I should do this at one o'clock in the morning, and having willed it, I went to sleep. Next Thursday, when I first met my friends, the elder lady told me that she woke up and saw my apparition advancing to her bedside. She screamed and woke her sisters, who also saw me." (The report includes the signed statement of the ladies, giving the time of the appearance, and the details thereof.)

"Again, on December 1, 1882, I was at Southall. At half-past nine I sat down to endeavor to fix my mind so strongly upon the interior of a house at

Kew, where Miss V. and her sister lived, that I seemed to be actually in the house. I was conscious, but was in a kind of mesmeric sleep. When I went to bed that night, I willed to be in the front bedroom of that house at Kew at twelve; and to make my presence felt by the inmates. Next day I went to Kew. Miss V.'s married sister told me, without any prompting from me, that she had seen me in the passage going from one room to another at half-past nine o'clock, and that at twelve, when she was wide awake, she saw me come to the front bedroom, where she slept, and take her hair, which is very long, into my hand. She said I then took her hand, and gazed into the palm intently. She said, 'You need not look at the lines, for I never have any trouble.' She then woke her sister. When Mrs. L. told me this, I took out the entry that I had made the previous night and read it to her. Mrs. L. is quite sure she was not dreaming. She had only seen me once before, two years previously. Again, on March 22, 1884, I wrote to Mr. Gurney, of the Psychical Research Society, telling him that I was going to make my presence felt by Miss V., at 44 Norland Square, at midnight. Ten days afterwards, I saw Miss V., when she voluntarily told me that on Saturday at midnight, she distinctly saw me, when she was quite wide awake."

The records of the psychic researchers are filled with numerous accounts of cases in which similar astral projections have occurred when the person was on his or her death-bed, but was still alive. It would seem that under such circumstances the astral senses are very much freer from the interference of the physical senses, and tend to manifest very strongly in the form of appearances to persons in whom the dying person is attached by the ties of affection. Many who read this course have known of cases of this kind, for they are of quite frequent occurrence.

The student will notice that in the majority of the cases cited in this chapter the clairvoyant has been in a state of sleep, or semi-sleep—often in a dream condition. But you must not jump to the conclusion that this condition is always necessary for the manifestation of this phenomenon. On the contrary, the advanced and well developed clairvoyants usually assume merely a condition of deep reverie or meditation, shutting out the sounds and thoughts of the physical plane, so as to be able to function better on the astral plane.

The reason that so many recorded cases have occurred when the clairvoyant person was asleep, and the vision appeared as a dream, is simply because in such a condition the physical senses of the person are stilled and at rest, and there is less likelihood of interference from them, and a better opportunity for the astral senses to function effectively. It is like the familiar cases in which one becomes so wrapped up in viewing a beautiful work of art, or in listening to a beautiful musical rendition, that he or she forgets all about the sights and sounds of the world outside. One sometimes gets into this same condition when reading an interesting book, or when witnessing an interesting play. When the psychic powers are concentrated upon any one channel of vision, the others fail to register a clear impression. The same rule holds good on the astral plane, as on the physical.

There are certain psychic conditions which are especially conducive to the manifestation of clairvoyant phenomena, as all students of the subject know very well. These conditions are somewhat hard to induce, at least until the clairvoyant has had considerable experience and practice. But, in the state of sleep, the person induces the desired conditions, in many cases, though he is not consciously doing so. As might naturally be expected, therefore, the majority of the recorded cases of clairvoyance have occurred when the clairvoyant person has been asleep.

I should also state, once more, that in many cases in which the clairvoyant has witnessed the "appearance" of another person, as in the cases such as I have just mentioned, there is always the possibility of the person having actually appeared in his astral body, unconsciously to himself of course. No one but a skilled occultist is able to distinguish between cases of this kind. The line between this class of clairvoyance and astral appearance is very thin, and, in fact, the two classes of phenomena shade and blend into each other. In reality, when one gets down to bottom principles, there is very little difference between the actual appearance in the astral body, and the strong projection of one's presence by means of will, conscious or unconscious, along the lines of awakening the clairvoyant vision of others. To attempt to explain the slight points of difference here, would only involve the student in a mass of technical description which would tend to confuse, rather than to enlighten him—from this I refrain.

LESSON - XI

CLAIRVOYANCE OF THE PAST

The third great class of clairvoyant phenomena, known as Time Clairvoyance, is divided into two sub-classes, as follows: (1) Past-Time Clairvoyance; and (2) Future-Time Clairvoyance. The characteristics of each of these sub-classes is indicated by its name.

Past-Time Clairvoyance, as indicated by the name, is that class of clairvoyant phenomena which is concerned with the perception of facts, events and happenings of past time. Whether the happening is that of five minutes ago, or of five thousand years ago, the principles involved are precisely the same. One is no more or less wonderful than is the other.

Many students confess themselves perplexed when they are first confronted with this class of phenomena. While they find it comparatively easy to see how by astral vision the clairvoyant is able to sense events happening at that moment, though thousands of miles away from the observer, they cannot at first understand how one can "see" a thing no longer in existence, but which disappeared from sight thousands of years ago. Naturally, they ask to be informed how this is possible, before proceeding to develop the faculty itself. Believing that this question is now being asked by you, the student of these lessons, I shall pause for a few moments and show you "just how" this wonderful thing becomes possible to the clairvoyant.

In the first place, it would undoubtedly be impossible to perceive a thing, even by astral vision, if it had entirely disappeared at some time in the past—this would be beyond all natural powers, astral as well as physical. But, as a matter of fact, the things of the past have not entirely disappeared, but, on the contrary, while having disappeared on the physical plane they still exist on the astral plane. I shall endeavor to explain this wonderful fact of nature to you in plain terms, although it belongs to one of the most mysterious classes of the occult facts of the universe.

In the occult teachings we find many references to "the Akashic Records," or what is sometimes called "the records of the Astral Light." Without going into technical occult definitions and explanations, I will say to you that the gist of this occult teaching is that in that high form of the universal substance which is called the Universal Ether there is found to be recorded all the happenings of the entire World Cycle of which the present time is a part. All that has happened from the very beginning of this World Cycle, millions of years ago, is preserved on these astral records, and may be read by the advanced clairvoyant or other person possessing occult powers of this kind. These records perish only with the termination of a World Cycle, which will not happen for millions of years yet to come.

To those who cannot accept the reasonableness of this occult fact, I would say that there are analogies to be found on other planes of natural manifestation. For instance, as astronomy teaches us, a star may be blotted out of existence, and yet its light will persist long after (perhaps until the end of world-time) traveling along at the rate of 186,000 miles each second. The light that we now see coming from the distant stars has left those stars many years ago—in some cases thousands of years ago. We see them not as they are now, but as they were at the time the ray of light left them, many years ago; The astronomers inform us that if one of these stars had been Transcribers Note: Text missing from original] sands) of years ago, we would still see it as in actual existence. In fact, it is believed that some of these stars which we see twinkling at night have actually been blotted out hundreds of years ago. We will not be aware of this fact until the light rays suddenly cease reaching us, after their journey of billions of miles and hundreds of years. A star blotted out of existence today would be seen by our children, and children's children.

The heat from a stove will be felt in a room long after the stove has been removed from it. A room will long contain the odor of something that has been removed from it. It is said that in one of the old mosques of Persia there may be perceived the faint odor of the musk that was exposed there hundreds of years ago—the very walls are saturated with the pungent odor. Again, is it not wonderful that our memories preserve the images of the sounds and forms which were placed there perhaps fifty years and more ago? How do these memory images survive and exist? Though we may have thought of the past thing for half a lifetime, yet, suddenly its image flashes into our consciousness. Surely this is as wonderful as the Akashic Records, though its "commonness" makes it lose its wonderful appearance to us.

Camille Flammarion, the eminent French astronomer, in a book written over twenty-five years ago, and which is now out of print, I believe, pictured a possible condition of affairs in which a disembodied soul would be able to perceive events that happened in the past, by simply taking a position in space in which he would be able to catch the light-waves that emanated from a distant planet at that particular time in the past the happenings of which he wanted to perceive. The little book was called "Lumen"—I advise you to read it, if you can find it in your public libraries.

Another writer has written somewhat along the same lines. I herewith give you a quotation from him, that you may get the idea he wishes to express—it will help you in your conception of the Akashic Records. He says: "When we see anything, whether it be the book we hold in our hands, or a star millions of miles away, we do so by means of a vibration in the ether, commonly called a ray of light, which passes from the object seen to our eyes. Now the speed with which this vibration passes is so great—about 186,000 miles in a second—that when we are considering any object in our own world we may regard it as practically instantaneous. When, however, we come to deal with interplanetary distances we have to take the speed of light into consideration, for an appreciable period is occupied in traversing these vast spaces. For example, it takes eight minutes and a quarter for light to travel to us from the sun, so that when we look at the solar orb we see it by means of a ray of light which left it more than eight minutes ago. From this follows a very curious result. The ray of light by which we see the sun can obviously report to us only the state of affairs' which existed in that luminary when it started on its journey, and would not be in the least affected by anything that happened after it left; so that we really see the sun not as it is, but as it was eight minutes ago. That is to say that if anything important took place in the sun—the formation of a new sun-spot, for instance—an astronomer who was watching the orb through his telescope at the time would be unaware of the incident while it was happening, since the ray of light bearing the news would not reach him until more than eight minutes later.

"The difference is more striking when we consider the fixed stars, because in their case the distances are so enormously greater. The pole star, for example, is so far off that light, traveling at the inconceivable speed above mentioned, takes a little more than fifty years to reach our eyes; and from that follows the strange but inevitable inference that we see the pole star not as or where it is at this moment, but as and where it was fifty years ago. Nay, if tomorrow some cosmic catastrophe were to shatter the pole star into fragments, we should still see it peacefully shining in the sky all the rest of our lives; our children would grow up to middle-age and gather their children about them in turn before the news of that tremendous accident reached any terrestial eye. In the same way there are other stars so far distant that light takes thousands of years to travel from them to us, and with reference to their condition our information is therefore thousands of years behind time. Now carry the argument a step farther. Suppose that we were able to place a man at the distance of 186,000 miles from the earth, and yet to endow him with the wonderful faculty of being able from that distance to see what was happening here as clearly as though he were still close beside us. It is evident that a man so placed would see everything a second after the time it really happened, and so at the present moment he would be seeing what happened a second ago. Double that distance, and he would be two seconds behind time, and so on; remove him to the distance of the sun (still allowing him to preserve the same mysterious power of sight) and he would look down and watch you doing not what you are doing now, but what you were doing eight minutes and a quarter ago. Carry him to the pole star, and he would see passing before his eyes the events of fifty years ago; he would be watching the childish gambols of those who at the same moment were really middle-aged men. Marvellous as this may sound, it is literally and scientifically true, and cannot be denied."

Flammarion, in his story, called "Lumen," makes his spirit hero pass at will along the ray of light from the earth, seeing the things of different eras of earth-time. He even made him travel backward along that ray, thus seeing the happenings in reverse order, as in a moving picture running backward. This story is of the greatest interest to the occultist, for while the Akashic Records are not the same as the light records, yet the analogy is so marked in many ways that the occultist sees here another exemplification of the old occult axiom that "as above, so below; as below, so above."

I take the liberty of quoting here from my little book, "The Astral World," in order to give you some further idea of the nature of these records in the Astral Light. The reader is supposed to be travelling in his astral body, having the phenomena of the astral pointed out to him by a competent occultist acting as his guide. The occultist-guide says to the student: "Changing our vibrations, we find ourselves entering a strange region, the nature of which you at first fail to discern. Pausing a moment until your astral vision becomes attuned to the peculiar vibrations of this region, you will find that you are becoming gradually aware of what may be called an immense picture gallery, spreading out in all directions, and apparently bearing a direct relation to every point of space on the surface of the earth. At first, you find it difficult to decipher the meaning of this great array of pictures. The trouble arises from the fact that they are arranged not one after the other in sequence on a flat plane; but rather in sequence, one after another, in a peculiar order which may be called the order of 'X-ness in space,' because it is neither the dimension of length, breadth, or depth—it is practically the order of the fourth dimension in space, which cannot be described in terms of ordinary spatial dimension. Again, you find upon closely examining the pictures that they are very minute—practically microscopic in size—and require the use of the peculiar magnifying power of astral vision to bring them up to a size capable of being recognized by your faculty of visual recognition.

"The astral vision, when developed, is capable of magnifying any object, material or astral, to an enormous degree—for instance, the trained occultist is able to perceive the whirling atoms and corpuscles of matter, by means of this peculiarity of astral vision. Likewise, he is able to plainly perceive many fine vibrations of light which are invisible to the ordinary sight. In fact, the peculiar Astral Light which pervades this region is due to the power of the astral vision to perceive and register these fine vibrations of light. Bring this power of magnifying into operation, and you will see that each of the little points and details of the great world picture so spread before you in the Astral Light is really a complete scene of a certain place on earth, at a certain period in the history of the earth. It resembles one of the small views in a series of moving pictures—a single view of a roll-film. It is fixed, and not in motion, and yet we can move forward along the fourth dimension, and thus obtain a moving picture of the history of any point on the surface of the earth, or even combine the various points into a large moving picture, in the same way. Let us prove this by actual experiment. Close your eyes for a moment, while we travel back in time (so to speak) along the series of these astral records—for, indeed, they travel back to the beginning of the history of the earth. Now open your eyes! Looking around you, you perceive the pictured representation of strange scenes filled with persons wearing a peculiar garb—but all is still, no life, no motion.

"Now, let us move forward in time, at much higher rate than that in which the astral views were registered. You now see flying before you the great movement of life on a certain point of space, in a far distant age. From birth to death you see the life of these strange people, all in the space of a few moments. Great battles are fought, and cities rise before your eyes, all in a great moving picture flying at a tremendous speed. Now stop, and then let us move backward in time, still gazing at the moving pictures. You see a strange sight, like that of 'reversing the film' in a moving picture. You see everything moving backward—cities crumbling into nothingness, men arising from their graves, and growing younger each second until they are finally born as babes—everything moving backward in time, instead of forward. You can thus witness any great historical event, or follow the career of any great personage from birth to death—or backward. You will notice, moreover, that everything is semi-transparent, and that accordingly you can see the picture of what is going on inside of buildings as well as outside of them. Nothing escapes the Astral Light Records. Nothing can be concealed from it. By traveling to any point in time, on the fourth dimension, you may begin at that point, and see a moving picture of the history of any part of the earth from that time to the present—or you may reverse the sequence by travelling backward, as we have seen. You may also travel in the Astral, on ordinary space dimensions, and thus see what happened simultaneously all over the earth, at any special moment of past-time, if you wish."

Now, I do not for a moment wish you to understand that the above experience is possible to every clairvoyant who is able to sense past-time events and happenings. On the contrary, the above experience is possible only to the advanced occultist, or to the student whom he may take with him on an astral trip, in the astral body. The clairvoyant merely catches glimpses of certain phases and fields of the great astral record region or state. For that matter, the ordinary clairvoyant merely sees a reflection of the true Astral-Light pictures—a reflection similar to that of a landscape reflected in a pond. Moreover, this reflection may be (and frequently is) disturbed as if by the ripples and waves of the pond in which the landscape is reflected. But, still, even the ordinary clairvoyant is able to secure results which are wonderful enough in all truth, and which far transcend the power of the person functioning on the physical plane alone.

Past-time clairvoyance is frequently induced by means of psychometry, in which the clairvoyant is able to have "the loose end" to unwind the ball of time. But, still, in some cases the clairvoyant is able to get en rapport with the astral records of past-time by the ordinary methods of meditation, etc. The main obstacle in the last mentioned case is the difficulty of coming in contact with the exact period of past-time sought for—in psychometry, the vibrations of the "associated object" supplies the missing-link.

Lacking the "associated object," the clairvoyant may obtain the link by bringing into the imagination some associated scene of that time—something else that happened about the same time. All that is needed is to get hold of something associated in space or in time with the sought for scene. All that is needed is the "loose end" of association. Sometimes the clairvoyant senses some past-time experience, the place and time of which is unknown to him. In such cases, it is necessary for him to get hold of some "loose end" by which he may work out the solution. For instance, the picture of a certain building or personage, or historical happening, may give the key to the mystery.

In very high forms of past-time clairvoyance, the clairvoyant is able not only to perceive the actual happenings of the past, but also to actually sense the thought and feelings of the actors therein—for these, too, are recorded on the astral plane. In other cases, the clairvoyant person is able to picture scenes and happenings relating to his past incarnations, even though he is not able to sense other past-time events and scenes. But, here again, many good past-time clairvoyants are not able to catch these glimpses of their own past lives, though able to perceive those of other persons. All these variations are due to certain technical differences into which I cannot go into detail at this place. Again some persons are able to perceive events that have happened to persons present before them, but are not able to contact past-time events in the ordinary way. There are a thousand-and-one variations in clairvoyant work. Only the highly advanced occultist is master of all of them. But, still every one may develop himself or herself, from humble beginnings.

In concluding this lesson, I wish to call your attention to the following advice from a man well advanced in the knowledge of the astral plane. He says: "It would be well for all students to bear in mind that occultism is the apotheosis of common-sense, and that every vision that comes to them is not necessarily a picture from the Akashic Records, nor every experience a revelation from on high. It is far better to err on the side of healthy skepticism, than of over-credulity, and it is an admirable rule never to hunt about for an occult explanation of anything when a plain and obvious physical one is available. Our duty is to endeaveor to keep our balance always, and never to lose our self-control, but to take a reasonable, common-sense view of whatever may happen to us, so that we may be wiser occultists, and more useful helpers than we have ever been before.

"We find examples of all degrees of the power to see into this 'memory of nature,' from the trained man who can consult the records for himself at will, down to the person who gets nothing but occasional vague glimpses, or has perhaps had only once such glimpse. But even the man who possesses this faculty only partially and occasionally still finds it of the deepest interest. The psychometer, who needs an object physically connected with the past in order to bring it all into life again around him; and the crystal-gazer who can sometimes direct his less certain astral telescope to some historic scene of long ago, may both derive the greatest enjoyment from the exercise of their respective gifts, even though they may not always understand exactly how their results are obtained, and may not have them fully under control under all circumstances.

"In many cases of the lower manifestations of these powers we find that they are exercised unconsciously. Many a crystal-gazer watches scenes from the past without being able to distinguish them from visions of the present. And many a vaguely-psychic person finds pictures constantly arising before his eyes, without ever realizing that he is in effect psychometrizing the various objects around him, as he happens to touch them or stand near them. An interesting variant of this class of psychics is the man who is able to psychometrize persons only, and not inanimate objects as is more usual. In most cases this faculty shows itself erratically, so that such a psychic will, when introduced to a stranger, often see in a flash some prominent event in that stranger's earlier life, but on similar occasions will receive no special impression. More rarely we meet with someone who gets detailed visions of the past life of nearly everyone whom he encounters. It may easily happen, moreover, that a person may see a picture of the past without recognizing it as such, unless there happens to be in it something which attracts special attention, such as a figure in armor, or in antique costume. Its probable, therefore, that occasional glimpses of these astral reflections of the akashic records are commoner than the published accounts would lead us to believe."

I would say to my students, make haste slowly. Do not try to rush development too rapidly. Perfect and develop yourself in one line of psychic power, before seeking another. Take things cooly, and do not lose your head because you happen to achieve some wonderful phenomena. Do not become conceited and vain-glorious. And, finally, do not prostitute your powers to ignoble ends, and make a cheap show of them. By cheapening and prostituting the higher psychic powers, the student frequently ends by losing them altogether. Moderation in all things is the safe policy. And it always is well for the occultist to resist temptation to use his powers for unworthy, sensational, or purely selfish purposes.

LESSON - XII

CLAIRVOYANCE OF THE FUTURE

Future-Time Clairvoyance, as indicated by its name, is that class of clairvoyant phenomena which is concerned with the perception of facts, events and happenings of future time. In this class of clairvoyant phenomena naturally fall all genuine cases of prophecy, prevision, foretelling, second-sight, etc. History, theological and secular, is filled with instances of the foretelling of the future by prophets, wise men, and others. By many, such powers are generally regarded as supernatural or divine. Without wishing to combat such theories and beliefs, I would say that the advanced occultists account for all such phenomena under the general laws of clairvoyance.

But while the phenomena itself is very well known, and is accepted as genuine in even many cases in which past-time clairvoyance is doubted, still it is even more difficult to explain than is past-time clairvoyance based on the Akashic Records or the Astral Light. To the person not well versed in occult knowledge, and esoteric principles, it is deemed impossible to intelligently account for the perception of an event before it has actually happened—perhaps years before its actual happening. While I cannot hope to make this matter absolutely clear to the person who is not an advanced student of occultism, still I shall try to throw at least some light on the underlying principles of this wonderful class of occult phenomena. The main point for the student to realize is that there are natural laws underlying this phenomenon, and that it is not a matter of supernatural power, or necessarily of divine special dispensation.

In the first place, in some of the simpler forms of future-time clairvoyance, there is merely a high development of subconscious reasoning from analogy. That is to say, the subconscious mental faculties of the person reason out that such-and-so being the case, then it follows that so-and-so will result, unless something entirely unexpected should prevent or intervene. This is merely an extension of certain forms of reasoning that we perform ordinarily. For instance, we see a child playing with a sharp tool, and we naturally reason that it will cut itself. We see a man acting in certain ways which generally lead to certain ends, and we naturally reason that the expected result will occur. The more experience that the observer has had, and the keener his faculty of perception and his power of deductive reasoning, the wider will be the range of his power in the direction of predicting future results from present happenings and conditions.

In this connection, we must remember that the ordinary clairvoyant has easier access to his subconscious mentality than has the average person. The subconscious mind perceives and notes many little things that the conscious mind overlooks, and therefore has better data from which to reason. Moreover, as all students of the subconscious know, these wonderful subconscious mental factulties have a very highly developed power of reasoning deductively from a given premise or fact. In fact, the subconscious faculties are almost perfect reasoning machines, providing they are supplied with correct data in the first place. Much of the so-called "intuitive reasoning" of persons arises from the operations of the subconscious mental faculties just mentioned.

But, you may say, this is very interesting, but it is not clairvoyance. Certainly, good student, but still clairvoyance plays an important part even in this elementary form of prevision and future-seeing. You must remember that by clairvoyant vision the real thoughts and feelings of a person may be perceived. But, unless the attention of the clairvoyant is specially directed to this, the conscious mind does not note it, and the matter reaches the subconscious faculties without interference or conscious knowledge on the part of the clairvoyant. This being so, it will be seen that the subconscious mind of the clairvoyant is able to reason deductively, in such cases, far beyond the power of even the subconscious mind of the ordinary person—it has fuller data and more complete material to work upon; of course.

It has become a proverb of the race that "coming events cast their shadows before"; and many persons frequently have little flashes of future-time seeing without realizing that they are really exercising elementary clairvoyant powers. The combination of even a simple form of clairvoyance and an active subconscious mind will often produce very wonderful results—although not of course the more complex phenomena of full clairvoyance and prevision. Some persons have claimed that even this form of prevision implies something like fate or predestination, but this is not fully true, for we must remember the fact that in some cases it is possible to so act in accordance with a clairvoyant warning of this kind that the impending calamity may be escaped. But, on the other hand, we must also remember that every event is the result of certain preceding events, without which it could not have happened, and which existing it must happen unless some new element intervenes. There is such a thing as cause and effect, we must remember—and if we can reason clearly from one to the other with sufficient clearness, then we may actually prophesy certain things in advance, always making allowance for the intervention of the unexpected.

An authority says on this phase of the question: "There is no doubt whatever that, just as what is happening now is the result of causes set in motion in the past, so what will happen in the future will be the result of causes already in operation. Even on this plane of life we can calculate that if certain actions are performed, certain results will follow; but our reckoning is constantly liable to be disturbed by the interference of factors which we have not been able to take into account. But if we raise our consciousness to the higher planes we can see much further into the results of our actions. We can trace, for example, the effect of a casual word, not only upon the person to whom it was addressed, but through him on many others as it is passed on in widening circles, until it seems to have affected the whole country; and one glimpse of such a vision is more efficient than any number of moral precepts in impressing upon us the necessity of extreme circumspection in thought, word, and deed. Not only can we from that plane see thus fully the result of every action, but we can also see where and in what way the results of other actions apparently quite unconnected with it will interfere with and modify it. In fact, it may be said that the results of all causes at present in action are clearly visible—that the future, as it would be if no entirely new causes should arise, lies open before our gaze.

"New causes of course do arise, because man's will is free; but in the case of all ordinary people the use which they make of their freedom may be calculated beforehand with considerable accuracy. The average man has so little real will that he is very much the creature of circumstances; his action in previous lives places him amid certain surroundings, and their influence upon him is so very much the most important factor in his life-story that his future course may be predicted with almost mathematical certainty. With the developed man the case is different; for him also the main events of life are arranged by his past actions, but the way in which he will allow them to affect him, the methods by which he will deal with them and perhaps triumph over them—these are all his own, and they cannot be foreseen even on the mental plane except as probabilities.

"Looking down on man's life in this way from above, it seems as though his free will could be exercised only in certain crises in his career. He arrives at a point in his life where there are obviously two or three alternative courses open before him; he is absolutely free to choose which of them he pleases, and although someone who knew his nature thoroughly well might feel almost certain what his choice would be, such knowledge on his friend's part is in no sense a compelling force. But when he has chosen, he has to go through with it and take the consequences; having entered upon a particular path he may, in many cases, be forced to go on for a very long time before he has any opportunity to turn aside. His position is somewhat like that of a driver of a train; when he comes to a junction he may have the points set either this way or that, and so can pass on to whichever line he pleases, but when he has passed on to one of them he is compelled to run on along the line which he has selected until he reaches another set of points, where again an opportunity of choice is offered to him."

But, interesting and wonderful as this phase of future-time clairvoyance undoubtedly is, it pales before the fuller and more complete phases. And, in the latter, we must look elsewhere for the explanation—or approach to an explanation. The explanation of this higher form of future-time clairvoyance must be looked for in a new conception of the nature and meaning of time. It is difficult to approach this question without becoming at once involved in technical metaphysical discussion. As an example of this difficulty, I invite you to consider the following from Sir Oliver Lodge, in his address to the British Association, at Cardiff, several years ago. While what he says is very clear to the mind of a person trained along these lines of subtle thought, it will be almost like Greek to the average person. Sir Oliver Lodge said:

"A luminous and helpful idea is that time is but a relative mode of regarding things; we progress through phenomena at a certain definite pace, and this subjective advance we interpret in an objective manner, as if events moved necessarily in this order and at this precise rate. But that may be only one mode of regarding them. The events may be in some sense of existence always, both past and future, and it may be we who are arriving at them, not they which are happening. The analogy of a traveller in a railway train is useful; if he could never leave the train nor alter its pace he would probably consider the landscapes as necessarily successive and be unable to conceive their co-existence * * * We perceive, therefore, a possible fourth dimensional aspect about time, the inexorableness of whose flow may be a natural part of our present limitations. And if we once grasp the idea that past and future may be actually existing, we can recognize that they may have a controlling influence on all present action, and the two together may constitute the 'higher plane' or totality of things after which, as it seems to me, we are impelled to seek, in connection with the directing of form or determinism, and the action of living being consciously directed to a definite and preconceived end."

Sir Oliver's illustration is somewhat akin to that of a person who sees a moving-picture show for the first time, and does not know how it is produced. To him it looks as if the events of the pictured story actually were developing and happening in time, whereas, in reality the whole picture is existing at one time. Its past, present and future is already pictured, and may be seen by one who knows the secret and how to look for the past or future scene; while, to the ordinary observer, the scene progresses in sequence, the present being followed by something else which is at this moment "in the future," and therefore, unknowable. To the senses of the ordinary observer only the present is in existence; while, in fact, the "future" is equally truly in existence at the same time, although not evident to the senses of the observer. Think over this a little, and let the idea sink into your mind—it may help you to understand something concerning the mystery of future-time clairvoyance, prevision, or second-sight.

Time, you know, is far more relative than we generally conceive it. It is a scientific fact that a person in the dream state may cover years of time in a dream that occupies only a few seconds of time. Persons have nodded and awakened immediately afterwards (as proved by others present in the room), and yet in that moment's time they have dreamed of long journeys to foreign lands, great campaigns of war, etc. Moreover, a loud sound (a pistol shot, for instance) which has awakened a sleeping person, has also set into effect a dream-state train of circumstances, constituting a long dream-state story which, after many events and happenings, terminated in the shot of a firing-squad—and then the man awoke. Now in this last mentioned case, not only has the dreamer experienced events covering a long time, all in the space of a second of time; but, also, the very sound which terminated the dream, also induced it from the very beginning—the last thing caused the first things to appear and proceed in sequence to the last! Persons under the influence of chloroform, or "laughing gas," have similar experiences—often the first sound heard at the moment of recovering consciousness seems to be the last thing in a long dream which preceded it, though the long dream was really caused by the final sound. Now, remember, that here not only did past, present and future exist at the same moment of time; but, also, the future caused the past and present to come into being.

On the physical plane, we have analogies illustrating this fact. It is said that in every acorn rests and exists, in miniature, the form of the future oak. And, some go so far as to say that the oak is the "ultimate cause" of the acorn—that the idea of the oak caused the acorn to be at all. In the same way, the "idea" of the man must be in the infant boy, from the moment of birth, and even from the moment of conception. But, let us pass on to the bold conception of the most advanced metaphysicians—they have a still more dazzling explanation, let us listen to it.

These occultists and metaphysicians who have thought long and deeply upon the ultimate facts and nature of the universe, have dared to think that there must exist some absolute consciousness—some absolute mind—which must perceive the past, present and future of the universe as one happening; as simultaneously and actively present at one moment of absolute time. They reason that just as man may see as one happening of a moment of his time some particular event which might appear as a year to some minute form of life and mind—the microscopic creatures in a drop of water, for instance; so that which seems as a year, or a hundred years, to the mind of man may appear as the happening of a single moment of a higher scale of time to some exalted Being or form of consciousness on a higher plane. You remember that it is said that "a thousand years is but as a day to the Lord;" and the Hindu Vedas tell us that "the creation, duration, and destruction of the universe, is as but the time of the twinkling of an eye to Brahman." I shall not proceed further along this line—I have given you a very strong hint here; you must work it out for yourself, if you feel so disposed. But there are certain consequences arising from this ultimate universal fact, which I must mention before passing on.

The high occult teachings hold that there is a plane of the higher astral world which may be said to carry a reflection of the Universal Mind—just as a lake contains a reflection of the distant mountain. Well, then, the clairvoyant vision at times is able to penetrate to the realm of that astral reflecting medium, and see somewhat dimly what is pictured there. As the future may be discerned in this reflected picture, by the clairvoyant mind, we see how future-seeing, prevision, and second-sight may be explained scientifically.

A writer has said: "On this plane, in some manner which down here is totally inexplicable, the past, the present, and the future, are all there existing simultaneously. One can only accept this fact, for its cause lies in the faculty of that exalted plane, and the way in which this higher faculty works is naturally quite incomprehensible to the physical brain. Yet now and then one may meet with a hint that seems to bring us a trifle nearer to a dim possibility of comprehension. When the pupil's consciousness is fully developed upon this higher plane, therefore, perfect prevision is possible to him, though he may not—nay, he certainly will not—be able to bring the whole result of his sight through fully and in order into his physical consciousness. Still, a great deal of clear foresight is obviously within his power whenever he likes to exercise it; and even when he is not exercising it, frequent flashes of foreknowledge come through into his ordinary life, so that he often has an instantaneous intuition as to how things will turn out."

The same writer says: "Short of perfect prevision we find that all degrees of this type of clairvoyance exist, from the occasional vague premonitions which cannot in any true sense be called sight at all, up to frequent and fairly complete second-sight. The faculty to which this latter somewhat misleading name has been given is an extremely interesting one, and would well repay more careful and systematic study than has hitherto been given to it. It is best known to us as a not infrequent possession of the Scottish Highlanders, though it is by no means confined to them. Occasional instances of it have appeared in almost every nation, but it has always been commonest among mountaineers and men of lonely life. With us in England it is often spoken of as if it were the exclusive appanage of the Celtic race, but in reality it has appeared among similarly situated peoples the world over, it is stated, for example, to be very common among the Westphalian peasantry.

"Sometimes the second-sight consists of a picture clearly foreshowing some coming event; more frequently, perhaps, the glimpse of the future is given in some symbolical appearance. It is noteworthy that the events foreseen are invariably unpleasant ones—death being the commonest of all; I do not recollect a single instance in which the second-sight has shown anything which was not of the most gloomy nature. It has a ghastly symbolism of its own—a symbolism of shrouds and corpse-candles, and other funeral horrors. In some cases it appears to be to a certain extent dependent upon locality, for it is stated that inhabitants of the Isle of Skye who possess the faculty often lose it when they leave the island, even though it be only to cross to the mainland. The gift of such sight is sometimes hereditary in a family for generations, but this is not an invariable rule, for it often appears sporadically in one member of a family otherwise free from its lugubrious influence.

"There may be still some people who deny the possibility of prevision, but such denial simply shows their ignorance of the evidence on the subject. The large number of authenticated cases leave no room for doubt as to the fact, but many of them are of such a nature as to render a reasonable explanation by no means easy to find. It is evident that the Ego possesses a certain amount of previsional faculty, and if the events foreseen were always of great importance, one might suppose that an extraordinary stimulus had enabled him for that occasion only to make a clear impression of what he saw upon his lower personality. No doubt that is the explanation of many of the cases in which death or grave disaster is foreseen, but there are a large number of instances on record to which it does not seem to apply, since the events foretold are frequently trivial and unimportant."

In the following chapter I shall present to your consideration some very remarkable cases of future-time clairvoyance, prevision, or second-sight; some of these are historical cases, and all are vouched for by the best authorities. I quote these cases not merely for their own interesting features, but also to give you an idea of how remarkable some of these instances are; and also to give you a clear conception of the way in which this form of clairvoyance tends to manifest itself.

Before passing on to these interesting cases, however, I wish to remind you that in future-time clairvoyance, as well as in past-time clairvoyance, the phenomenon may be manifested in many ways and according to several methods. That is to say, that in future-time clairvoyance the vision may come in the state of meditation or reverie; it may come along the lines of psychometry, some associated object or person supplying the connecting link; or, again, it may come as the result of crystal-gazing, etc. This is as we might naturally expect, for this form of clairvoyance is merely one special and particular phase of clairvoyance in general, and of course, comes under the general laws and rules governing all clairvoyant phenomena.

Future-time clairvoyance, prevision and second-sight may, like any other form of clairvoyance, be developed and unfolded, by means of the same rules and methods that I have already suggested to you in the preceding lessons. It is all a matter of attention, application, patience, exercise and practice. I may say, however, that the strong desire and wish for the perception of future events, held firmly in mind during the practicing and exercising, will tend to unfold and develop the clairvoyant faculties in this particular direction. Strong desire, and earnest attention in the desired direction, will do much to cultivate, develop and unfold any psychic faculty.

Just as meditation and reverie about past times and things tend to develop past-time clairvoyance, so will meditation and reverie about future time and things tend to develop prevision and the seeing of future things. This, indeed, is the very first step toward the attainment of this form of clairvoyance. The attention clears the psychic path, over which the astral faculties travel. In the astral, as on the physical, the rule is: always look where you are going—look ahead on the path over which you wish to travel.

LESSON - XIII

SECOND-SIGHT, PREVISION, ETC.

Notwithstanding the difficulties in the way of an intelligent explanation of the phenomena of future-time clairvoyance, second-sight, prevision, etc., of which I have spoken in the preceding lesson, the human race has always had a lively reminder of the existence of such phenomena; and the records of the race have always contained many instances of the manifestation thereof. Among all peoples, in all lands, in all times, there have been noted remarkable instances of the power of certain persons to peer into, and correctly report from, the mysterious regions of the future. Passing from the traditional reports of the race, and the minor instances known to almost every person, we find that the scientific investigators of psychic phenomena have gathered together an enormous array of well authenticated cases of this class. The reports of the Society for Psychical research contain hundreds of such cases, which the student may read and study with interest and profit.

It is not my intention to present a full history of the reports of this character. Rather, I shall call your attention to a few striking cases, in order to illustrate the phenomenon clearly and forcibly. There is such a wealth of material of this kind that it embarrases one who wishes to select from it. However, I shall do the best I can in that direction. Following, to commence with, I give you extracts from a well known case reported by a prominent member of the Theosophical Society, which has attracted much attention. It was related to this person by one of the actors in the scene. It happened in India. A party of English army officers was entering a dense jungle. Then follows the story, as below:

"We plunged into the jungle, and had walked on for about an hour without much success, when Cameron, who happened to be next to me, stopped suddenly, turned pale as death, and, pointing straight before him, cried in accents of horror: 'See! see! merciful heavens, look there!' 'Where? what? what is it?' we all shouted confusedly, as we rushed up to him, and looked around in expectation of encountering a tiger—a cobra—we hardly knew what, but assuredly something terrible, since it had been sufficient to cause such evident emotion in our usually self-contained comrade. But neither tiger nor cobra was visible—nothing but Cameron pointing with ghastly haggard face and starting eyeballs at something we could not see.

"'Cameron! Cameron!' cried I, seizing his arm, 'for heavens sake speak! What is the matter?' Scarcely were the words out of my mouth when a low but very peculiar sound struck upon my ear, and Cameron, dropping his pointing hand, said in a hoarse, strained voice, 'There! you heard it? Thank God it's over!' and fell to the ground insensible. There was a momentary confusion while we unfastened his collar, and I dashed in his face some water which I fortunately had in my flask, while another tried to pour brandy between his clenched teeth; and under cover of it I whispered to the man next to me (one of our greatest skeptics, by the way), 'Beauchamp, did you hear anything?' 'Why, yes,' he replied, 'a curious sound, very; a sort of crash or rattle far away in the distance, yet very distinct; if the thing were not utterly impossible, I could have sworn that it was the rattle of musketry.' 'Just my impression,' murmured I; 'but hush! he is recovering.'

"In a minute or two he was able to speak feebly, and began to thank us and apologize for giving trouble; and soon he sat up, leaning against a tree, and in a firm, though low voice said: 'My dear friends, I feel that I owe you an explanation of my extraordinary behavior. It is an explanation that I would fain avoid giving; but it must come some time, and so may as well be given now. You may perhaps have noticed that when during our voyage you all joined in scoffing at dreams, portents and visions, I invariably avoided giving any opinion on the subject. I did so because, while I had no desire to court ridicule or provoke discussion, I was unable to agree with you, knowing only too well from my own dread experience that the world which men agree to call that of the supernatural is just as real as—nay, perhaps even more real than—this world we see about us. In other words, I, like many of my countrymen, am cursed with the gift of second-sight—that awful faculty which foretells in vision calamities that are shortly to occur.

"'Such a vision I had just now, and its exceptional horror moved me as you have seen. I saw before me a corpse—not that of one who has died a peaceful, natural death, but that of the victim of some terrible accident; a ghastly, shapeless mass, with a face swollen, crushed, unrecognizable. I saw this dreadful object placed in a coffin, and the funeral service performed over it. I saw the burial-ground, I saw the clergyman: and though I had never seen either before, I can picture both perfectly in my mind's eye now; I saw you, myself, Beauchamp, all of us and many more, standing round as mourners; I saw the soldiers raise their muskets after the service was over; I heard the volley they fired—and then I knew no more.' As he spoke of that volley of musketry I glanced across with a shudder at Beauchamp, and the look of stony horror on that handsome skeptic's face was not to be forgotten."

Omitting the somewhat long recital of events which followed, I would say that later in the same day the party of young officers and soldiers discovered the body of their commanding officer in the shocking condition so vividly and graphically described by young Cameron. The story proceeds as follows:

"When, on the following evening, we arrived at our destination, and our melancholy deposition had been taken down by the proper authorities, Cameron and I went out for a quiet walk, to endeavor with the assistance of the soothing influence of nature to shake off something of the gloom which paralyzed our spirits. Suddenly he clutched my arm, and, pointing through some rude railings, said in a trembling voice, 'Yes, there it is! that is the burial-ground of yesterday.' And, when later on we were introduced to the chaplain of the post, I noticed, though my friends did not, the irrepressible shudder with which Cameron took his hand, and I knew that he had recognized the clergyman of his vision."

The story concludes with the statement that in all the little details, as well as the main points, the scene at the burial of the commanding officer corresponded exactly with the vision of Cameron. This story brings out the fact that the Scotch people are especially given to manifestations of second-sight—particularly the Highlanders or mountain people of that land. It is hard to find a Scotchman, who, in his heart, does not believe in second-sight, and who has not known of some well authenticated instance of its manifestation. In other lands, certain races, or sub-races, seem to be specially favored (or cursed, as Cameron asserted) with this power. It will be noticed, usually, that such people dwell, or have dwelt in the highlands or mountains of their country. There seems to be something in the mountains and hills which tends to develop and encourage this power in those dwelling among them. The story is also remarkable in the fact that the impression was so strong in the mind of Cameron that it actually communicated itself by clairaudience to those near to him—this is quite unusual, though not without correspondence in other cases. Otherwise, the case is merely a typical one, and may be duplicated in the experience of thousands of other men and women.

George Fox, the pioneer Quaker, had this faculty well developed, and numerous instances of its manifestation by him are recorded. For instance, he foretold the death of Cromwell, when he met him riding at Hampton Court; he said that he felt "a waft of death" around and about Cromwell; and Cromwell died shortly afterwards. Fox also publicly foretold the dissolution of the Rump Parliament of England; the restoration of Charles II; and the Great Fire of London—these are historical facts, remember. For that matter, history contains many instances of this kind: the prophecy of Caesar's death, and its further prevision by his wife, for instance. The Bible prophecies and predictions, major and minor, give us semi-historical instances.

A celebrated historical instance of remarkable second-sight and prevision, is that of Cazotte, whose wonderful prediction and its literal fulfilment are matters of French history. Dumas has woven the fact into one of his stories, in a dramatic manner—but even so he does not make the tale any more wonderful than the bare facts. Here is the recital of the case by La Harpe, the French writer, who was a personal witness of the occurrence, and whose testimony was corroborated by many others who were present at the time. La Harpe says:

"It appears as but yesterday, and yet, nevertheless, it was at the beginning of the year 1788. We were dining with one of our brethren at the Academy—a man of considerable wealth and genius. The conversation became serious; much admiration was expressed on the revolution in thought which Voltaire had effected, and it was agreed that it was his first claim to the reputation he enjoyed. We concluded that the revolution must soon be consummated; that it was indispensible that superstition and fanaticism should give way to philosophy, and we began to calculate the probability of the period when this should be, and which of the present company should live to see it. The oldest complained that they could scarcely flatter themselves with the hope; the younger rejoiced that they might entertain this very probable expectation; and they congratulated the Academy especially for having prepared this great work, and for having been the rallying point, the centre, and the prime mover of the liberty of thought.

"One only of the guests had not taken part in all the joyousness of this conversation, and had even gently and cheerfully checked our splendid enthusiasm. This was Cazotte, an amiable and original man, but unhappily infatuated with the reveries of the illumaniti. He spoke, and with the most serious tone, saying: 'Gentleman, be satisfied; you will all see this great and sublime revolution, which you so much desire. You know that I am a little inclined to prophesy; I repeat, you will see it,' He was answered by the common rejoinder: 'One need not be a conjuror to see that.' He answered: 'Be it so; but perhaps one must be a little more than conjuror for what remains for me to tell you. Do you know what will be the consequences of this revolution—what will be the consequence to all of you, and what will be the immediate result—the well-established effect—the thoroughly recognized consequences to all of you who are here present?'

"'Ah' said Condorcet, with his insolent and half-suppressed smile, 'let us hear—a philosopher is not sorry to encounter a prophet—let us hear!' Cazotte replied: 'You, Monsier de Condorcet—you will yield up your last breath on the floor of a dungeon; you will die from poison, which you will have taken in order to escape from execution—from poison which the happiness of that time will oblige you to carry about your person. You, Monsieur de Chamfort, you will open your veins with twenty-two cuts of a razor, and yet will not die till some months afterward.' These personages looked at each other, and laughed again. Cazotte continued: 'You, Monsieur Vicq d'Azir, you will not open your own veins, but you will cause yourself to be bled six times in one day, during a paroxysm of the gout, in order to make more sure of your end, and you will die in the night.'

"Cazotte went on: 'You, Monsieur de Nicolai, you will die on the scaffold; you, Monsieur Bailly, on the scaffold; you, Monsieur de Malesherbes, on the scaffold. 'Ah, God be thanked,' exclaimed Roucher, 'and what of I?' Cazotte replied: 'You? you also will die on the scaffold.' 'Yes,' replied Chamfort, 'but when will all this happen?' Cazotte answered: 'Six years will not pass over, before all that I have said to you shall be accomplished.' Here I (La Harpe) spoke, saying: 'Here are some astonishing miracles, but you have not included me in your list.' Cazotte answered me, saying: 'But you will be there, as an equally extraordinary miracle; you will then be a Christian!' Vehement exclamations on all sides followed this startling assertion. 'Ah!' said Chamfort, 'I am conforted; if we shall perish only when La Harpe shall be a Christian, we are immortal;'

"Then observed Madame la Duchesse de Grammont: 'As for that, we women, we are happy to be counted for nothing in these revolutions: when I say for nothing, it is not that we do not always mix ourselves up with them a little; but it is a received maxim that they take no notice of us, and of our sex.' 'Your sex, ladies' said Cazotte, 'your sex will not protect you this time; and you had far better meddle with nothing, for you will be treated entirely as men, without any difference whatever.' 'But what, then, are you really telling us of Monsieur Cazotte? You are preaching to us the end of the world.' 'I know nothing on that subject; but what I do know is, that you Madame la Duchesse, will be conducted to the scaffold, you and many other ladies with you, in the cart of the executioner, and with your hands tied behind your backs. 'Ah! I hope that in that case, I shall at least have a carriage hung in black.' 'No, madame; higher ladies than yourself will go, like you, in the common car, with their hands tied behind them.' 'Higher ladies! what! the princesses of the blood?' 'Yea, and still more exalted personages!' replied Cazotte.

"Here a sensible emotion pervaded the whole company, and the countenance of the host was dark and lowering—they began to feel that the joke was becoming too serious. Madame de Grammont, in order to dissipate the cloud, took no notice of the reply, and contented herself with saying in a careless tone: 'You see, that he will not leave me even a confessor!' 'No, madame!' replied Cazotte, 'you will not have one—neither you, nor any one besides. The last victim to whom this favor will be afforded will be—' Here he stopped for a moment. 'Well! who then will be the happy mortal to whom this prerogative will be given?' Cazotte replied: 'It is the only one which he will have then retained—and that will be the King of France!'" This last startling prediction caused the company to disband in something like terror and dismay, for the mere mention of such thing was akin to treason.

The amazing sequel to this strange story is that within the six years allotted by the prophecy, every detail thereof was verified absolutely. The facts are known to all students of the French Revolution, and may be verified by reference to any history of that terrible period. To appreciate the startling nature of the prophecy when made, one needs but to be acquainted with the position and characteristics of the persons whose destinies were foretold. This celebrated instance of highly advanced future-time clairvoyance, or prevision, has never been equalled. The reason, perhaps, is that Cazotte indeed was an advanced and highly developed occultist—the account mentions this, you will notice. This class of persons very seldom prophecy in this way, for reasons known to all occultists. The ordinary cases recorded are those in which the manifestation is that of a person of lesser powers and less perfect development.

Advanced occultists know the danger of a careless use of this power. They know that (omitting other and very important reasons) such revelations would work a terrible effect upon the minds of persons not sufficiently well balanced to stand the disclosure. Moreover, they know that if the average person knew the principal details of his future life on earth, then he would lose interest in it—it would become stale and would lose the attraction of the unknown. In such a case, the pleasant things to come would lose their attractiveness by reason of having been dwelt on so long that their flavor was lost; and the unpleasant things would become unbearable by reason of the continual anticipation of them. We are apt to discount our pleasures by dwelling too much upon them in anticipation; and, as we all know, the dread of a coming evil often is worse than the thing itself—we suffer a thousand pangs in anticipation to one in reality. But, as I have intimated, there are other, and still more serious reasons why the advanced occultists do not indulge in public prophecies of this kind. It is probable that Cazotte decided to, and was permitted to, make his celebrated prophecy for some important occult reason of which La Harpe had no knowledge—it doubtless was a part of the working out of some great plan, and it may have accomplished results undreamed of by us. At any rate, it was something very much out of the; ordinary, even in the case of advanced occultists and masters of esoteric knowledge.

Another case which has a historic value is the well-known case concerning the assassination of Spencer Perceval, the Chancellor of the Exchequer, in England, which occurred in the lobby of the House of Commons. The persons who have a knowledge of the case report that some nine days before the tragic occurrence a Cornish mine manager, named John Williams, had a vision, three times in succession, in which he saw a small man, dressed in a blue coat and white waistcoat, enter the lobby of the House of Commons; whereupon another man, dressed in a snuff-colored coat, stepped forward, and, drawing a pistol from an inside pocket fired at and shot the small man, the bullet lodging in the left breast. In the vision, Williams turned and asked some bystander the name of the victim; the bystander replied that the stricken man was Mr. Spencer Perceval, the Chancellor of the Exchequer. The valuable feature of the case, from a scientific standpoint, lies in the fact that Williams was very much impressed by his thrice-repeated vision, and was greatly disturbed thereby. His anxiety was so great that he spoke of the matter to several friends, and asked them whether it would not be well for him to go to London for the purpose of warning Mr. Perceval. His friends ridiculed the whole matter, and persuaded him to give up the idea of visiting London for the purpose named. Those who had a knowledge of the vision were greatly startled and shocked when several days afterward the assassination occurred, agreeing in perfect detail with the vision of the Cornishman. The case, vouched for as it was by a number of reliable persons who had been consulted by Williams, attracted much attention at the time, and has since passed into the history of remarkable instances of prevision.

In some cases, however, the prevision seems to come as a warning, and in many cases the heeding of the warning has prevented the unpleasant features from materializing as seen in the vision. Up to the point of the action upon the warning the occurrence agree perfectly with the vision—but the moment the warned person acts so as to prevent the occurrence, the whole train of circumstances is broken. There is an occult explanation of this, but it is too technical to mention at this place.

What is known to psychic researchers as "the Hannah Green case" is of this character. This story, briefly, is that Hannah Green, a housekeeper of Oxfordshire, dreamt that she, having been left alone in the house of a Sunday evening, heard a knock at the door. Opening the door she found a tramp who tried to force his way into the house. She struggled to prevent his entrance, but he struck her with a bludgeon and rendered her insensible, whereupon he entered the house and robbed it. She related the vision to her friends, but, as nothing happened for some time, the matter almost passed from her mind. But, some seven years afterward, she was left in charge of the house on a certain Sunday evening; during the evening she was startled by a sudden knock at the door, and her former vision was recalled to her memory quite vividly. She refused to go to the door, remembering the warning, but instead went up to a landing on the stair and looked out the window, she saw at the door the very tramp whom she had seen in the vision some seven years before, armed with a bludgeon and striving to force an entrance into the house. She took steps to frighten away the rascal, and she was saved from the unpleasant conclusion of her vision. Many similar cases are recorded.

In some cases persons have been warned by symbols of various kinds; or else have had prevision in the same way. For instance, many cases are known in which the vision is that of the undertaker's wagon standing before the door of the person who dies sometime afterward. Or, the person is visioned clad in a shroud. The variations of this class are innumerable. Speak to the average dweller in the highlands of Scotland, or certain counties in Ireland, regarding this—you will be furnished with a wealth of illustrations and examples.

This phase of the general subject of clairvoyance is very fascinating to the student and investigator, and is one in which the highest psychic or astral powers of sensing are called into play. In fact, as I have said, there is here a reflection of something very much higher than the astral or psychic planes of being. The student catches a glimpse of regions infinitely higher and grander. He begins to realize at least something of the existence of that Universal Consciousness "in which we live, and move, and have our being;" and of the reality of the Eternal Now, in which past, present and future are blended as one fact of infinite consciousness. He sees the signboard pointing to marvelous truths!

LESSON - XIV

ASTRAL-BODY TRAVELING

There is much confusion existing in the minds of the average students of occultism concerning the distinction between astral visioning by means of the astral senses in clairvoyance, and the visioning of the astral senses during the travels of the astral body away from the physical body. There is such a close connection between the two several phases of occult phenomena that it is easy to mistake one for the other; in fact, there is often such a blending of the two that it is quite difficult to distinguish between them. However, in this lesson I shall endeavor to bring out the characteristics of astral body visioning, that the student may learn to distinguish them from those of the ordinary clairvoyant astral visioning, and recognize them when he experiences them.

The main points of distinction are these: When visioning clairvoyantly by means of the astral senses, as described in the preceding chapters of this book, the clairvoyant usually perceives the scene, person or event as a picture on a flat surface. It is true that there is generally a perfect perspective, similar to that of a good stereoscopic view, or that of a high-grade moving picture photograph—the figures "stand out," and do not appear "flat" as in the case of an ordinary photograph; but still at the best it is like looking at a moving picture, inasmuch as the whole scene is all in front of you. Visioning in the astral body, on the contrary, gives you an "all around" view of the scene. That is to say, in such case you see the thing just as you would were you there in your physical body—you see in front of you; on the sides of you, out of the corner of your eye; if you turn your head, you may see in any direction; and you may turn around and see what is happening behind you. In the first case you are merely gazing at an astral picture in front of you; while in the second place you are **Actually There in Person.**

There are some limitations to this "seeing all around" when in the astral body, however, which I should note in passing. For instance, if when in the astral body you examine the akashic records of the past, or else peer into the scenes of the future, you will see these things merely as a picture, and will not be conscious of being present personally in the scene. (An apparent exception is to be noted here, also, viz., if your past-time visioning includes the perception of yourself in a former incarnation, you may be conscious of living and acting in your former personality; again, if you are psychometrizing from fossil remains, or anything concerned with a living creature of the past, you may "take on" the mental or emotional conditions of that creature, and seem to sense things from the inside, rather than from the outside. This, of course, is also a characteristic of the ordinary clairvoyant vision of the past.) But when, in the astral body, you perceive a present-time scene in space, you are, to all intents and purposes, an actual participant—you are actually present at the place and time. The sense of "being actually present in the body" is the leading characteristic of the astral body visioning, and distinguishes it from the "picture seeing" sensing of ordinary clairvoyance. This is stating the matter is as plain and simple form as is possible, ignoring many technical details and particulars.

You, being a student of occultism, of course know that the astral body is a fine counterpart of the physical body, composed of a far more subtle form of substance than is the latter, that under certain conditions you may travel in your astral body, detached from your physical body (except being connected with it with a slender astral cord, bearing a close resemblance to the umbilical cord which connects the newborn babe with the placenta in the womb of its mother), and explore the realms of the astral plane. This projection of the astral body, as a rule, occurs only when the physical body is stilled in sleep, or in trance condition. In fact, the astral body frequently is projected by us during the course of our ordinary sleep, but we fail to remember what we have seen in our astral journeys, except, occasionally, dim flashes of partial recollection upon awakening. In some cases, however, our astral visioning is so distinct and vivid, that we awaken with a sense of having had a peculiar experience, and as having actually been out of the physical body at the time.

In some cases, the person traveling in the astral is able to actually take part in the distant scene, and may, under certain circumstances actually materialize himself so as to be seen by persons in their physical bodies. I am speaking now, of course, of the untrained person. The trained and developed occultist, of course, is able to do these things deliberately and consciously, instead of unconsciously and without intention as in the case of the ordinary person. I shall quote here from another writer on the subject, whose point of view, in connection with my own, may serve to bring about a clear understanding in the mind of the student—it is always well to view any subject from as many angles as possible. This writer says:

"We enter here upon an entirely new variety of clairvoyance, in which the consciousness of the seer no longer remains in or closely connected with his physical body, but is definitely transferred to the scene which he is examining. Though it has no doubt greater dangers for the untrained seer than either of the other methods, it is yet quite the most satisfactory form of clairvoyance open to him. In this case, the man's body is either asleep or in a trance, and its organs are consequently not available for use while the vision is going on, so that all description of what is seen, and all questioning as to further particulars, must be postponed until the wanderer returns to this plane. On the other hand, the sight is much fuller and more perfect; the man hears as well as sees everything which passes before him, and can move about freely at will within the very wide limits of the astral plane. He has also the immense advantage of being able to take part, as it were, in the scenes which come before his eyes—of conversing at will with various entities on the astral plane, and from whom so much information that is curious and interesting may be obtained. If in addition he can learn how to materialize himself (a matter of no great difficulty for him when once the knack is acquired), he will be able to take part in physical events or conversations at a distance, and to show himself to an absent friend at will.

"Again, he will have the additional power of being able to hunt about for what he wants. By means of the other varieties of clairvoyance, for all practical purposes he may find a person or place only when he is already acquainted with it; or, when he is put en rapport with it by touching something physically connected with it, as in psychometry. By the use of the astral body, however, a man can move about quite freely and rapidly in any direction, and can (for example) find without difficulty any place pointed out upon a map, without either any previous knowledge of the spot or any object to establish a connection with it. He can also readily rise high into the air so as to gain a bird's eye view of the country which he is examining, so as to observe its extent, the contour of its coastline, or its general character. Indeed, in every way his power and freedom are far greater when he uses this method than they are in any of the lesser forms of clairvoyance."

In many well authenticated cases, we may see that the soul of a dying person, one whose physical end is approaching, visits friends and relatives in the astral body, and in many cases materializes and even speaks to them. In such cases the dying person accomplishes the feat of astral manifestation without any special occult knowledge; the weakened links between the physical and the higher phases of the soul render the temporary passing-out comparatively easy, and the strong desire of the dying person furnishes the motive power necessary. Such visits, however, are often found to be merely the strongly charged thought of the dying person, along the lines of telepathy, as I have previously explained to you. But in many cases there can be no doubt that the phenomenon is a clear case of astral visitation and materialization.

The records of the Society for Psychical Research contain many instances of this kind; and similar instances are to be found in other records of psychical research. I shall quote a few of these cases for you, that you may get a clear idea of the characteristics thereof. Andrew Lang, an eminent student and investigator along the lines of the psychic and occult, gives us the following case, of which he says, "Not many stories have such good evidence in their favor." The story as related by Mr. Lang in one of his books is as follows:

"Mary, the wife of John Goffe of Rochester, being afflicted with a long illness, removed to her father's house at West Mailing, about nine miles from her own. The day before her death she grew very impatiently desirous to see her two children, whom she had left at home to the care of a nurse. She was too ill to be moved, and between one and two o'clock in the morning she fell into a trance. One widow, Turner, who watched with her that night, says that her eyes were open and fixed, and her jaw fallen. Mrs. Turner put her hand to her mouth, but could perceive no breath. She thought her to be in a fit, and doubted whether she were dead or alive. The next morning the dying woman told her mother that she had been at home with her children, saying, 'I was with them last night when I was asleep.'

"The nurse at Rochester, widow Alexander by name, affirms that a little before two o'clock that morning she saw the likeness of the said Mary Goffe come out of the next chamber (where the elder child lay in a bed by itself), the door being left open, and stood by her bedside for about a quarter of an hour; the younger child was there lying by her. Her eyes moved and her mouth went, but she said nothing. The nurse, moreover says that she was perfectly awake; it was then daylight, being one of the longest days of the year. She sat up in bed and looked steadfastly on the apparition. In that time she heard the bridge clock strike two, and a while after said: 'In the name of the Father, Son and Holy Ghost, what art thou?' Thereupon the apparition removed and went away; she slipped out of her clothes and followed, but what became on't she cannot tell."

In the case just mentioned, Mr. Lang states that the nurse was so frightened that she was afraid to return to bed. As soon as the neighbors were up and about she told them of what she had seen; but they told her that she had been dreaming. It was only when, later on, news came of what had happened at the other end of the line—the bedside of the dying woman, that they realized just what had happened.

In a work by Rev. F.G. Lee, there are several other cases of this kind quoted, all of which are stated by Mr. Lee to be thoroughly well authenticated. In one of the cases a mother, when dying in Egypt, appears to her children in Torquay, and is clearly seen in broad daylight by all five children and also by the nursemaid. In another, a Quaker lady dying at Cockermouth is clearly seen and recognized in daylight by her three children at Seattle, the remainder of the story being almost identical with that of the Goffe case just quoted.

In the records of the Society for Psychical Research, the following case appears, the person reporting it being said to be of good character and reputation for truthfulness and reliability. The story is as follows: "One morning in December, 1836, A. had the following dream, or he would prefer to call it, revelation. He found himself suddenly at the gate of Major N.M.'s avenue, many miles from his home. Close to him was a group of persons, one of whom was a woman with a basket on her arm, the rest were men, four of whom were tenants of his own, while the others were unknown to him. Some of the strangers seemed to be assaulting H.W., one of his tenants, and he interfered. A. says, 'I struck violently at the man on my left, and then with greater violence at the man's face on my right. Finding, to my surprise, that I had not knocked down either, I struck again and again with all the violence of a man frenzied at the sight of my poor friend's murder. To my great amazement I saw my arms, although visible to my eye, were without substance, and the bodies of the men I struck at and my own came close together after each blow, through the shadowy arms I struck with. My blows were delivered with more extreme violence than I ever think I exerted, but I became painfully convinced of my incompetency. I have no consciousness of what happened after this feeling of unsubstantiality came upon me.'

"Next morning, A. experienced the stiffness and soreness of violent bodily exercise, and was informed by his wife that in the course of the night he had much alarmed her by striking out again and again in a terrific manner, 'as if fighting for his life.' He, in turn, informed her of his dream, and begged her to remember the names of those actors in it who were known to him. On the morning of the following day (Wednesday) A. received a letter from his agent, who resided in the town close to the scene of the dream, informing him that his tenant had been found on Tuesday morning at Major N.M.'s gate, speechless and apparently dying from a fracture of the skull, and that there was no trace of the murderers.

"That night A. started for the town, and arrived there on Thursday morning. On his way to a meeting of magistrates, he met the senior magistrate of that part of the country, and requested him to give orders for the arrest of the three men whom, besides H.W., he had recognized in his dream, and to have them examined separately. This was at once done. The three men gave identical accounts of the occurrence, and all named the woman who was with them. She was then arrested and gave precisely similar testimony. They said that between eleven and twelve on the Monday night they had been walking homewards altogether along the road, when they were overtaken by three strangers, two of whom savagely assaulted H.W., while the other prevented his friends from interfering. H.W. did not die, but was never the same man afterwards; he subsequently emigrated."

Stead, the English editor and psychical researcher, relates the following case, which he accepts as truthful and correct, after careful investigation of the circumstances and of the character and reputation of the person relating it. The story proceeds as follows:

"St. Eglos is situated about ten miles from the Atlantic, and not quite so far from the old market town of Trebodwina. Hart and George Northey were brothers, and from childhood their lives had been marked by the strongest brotherly affection. Hart and George Northey had never been separated from their birth until George became a sailor, Hart meantime joining his father in business. On the 8th of February, 1840, while George Northey's ship was lying in port at St. Helena, he had the following strange dream:

"Last night I dreamt that my brother was at Trebodwina Market, and that I was with him, quite close by his side, during the whole of the market transactions. Although I could see and hear which passed around me, I felt sure that it was not my bodily presence which thus accompanied him, but my shadow or rather my spiritual presence, for he seemed quite unconscious that I was near him. I felt that my being thus present in this strange way betokened some hidden danger which he was destined to meet, and which I know my presence could not avert, for I could not speak to warn him of his peril."

The story then proceeds to relate how Hart collected considerable money at Trebodwina Market, and then started to ride homeward. George tells what happened to his brother on the way, as follows:

"My terror gradually increased as Hart approached the hamlet of Polkerrow, until I was in a perfect frenzy, frantically desirous, yet unable to warn my brother in some way and prevent him from going further. I suddenly became aware of two dark shadows thrown across the road. I felt that my brother's hour had come, and I was powerless to aid him! Two men appeared, whom I instantly recognized as notorious poachers who lived in a lonely wood near St. Eglos. They wished him 'Good night, mister!' civilly enough. He replied, and entered into conversation with them about some work he had promised them. After a few minutes they asked him for some money. The elder of the two brothers, who was standing near the horse's head, said: 'Mr. Northey, we know you have just come from Trebodwina Market with plenty of money in your pockets; we are desperate men, and you bean't going to leave this place until we've got that money; so hand over!' My brother made no reply except to slash at him with the whip, and spur the horse at him.

"The younger of the ruffians instantly drew a pistol, and fired. Hart dropped lifeless from the saddle, and one of the villains held him by the throat with a grip of iron for some minutes, as thought to make assurance doubly sure, and crush out any particle of life my poor brother might have left. The murderers secured the horse to a tree in the orchard, and, having rifled the corpse, they dragged it up the stream, concealing it under the overhanging banks of the water-course. Then they carefully covered over all marks of blood on the road, and hid the pistol in the thatch of a disused hut close to the roadside; then, setting the horse free to gallop home alone, they decamped across the country to their own cottage."

The story then relates how George Northey's vessel left St. Helena the next day after the dream, and reached Plymouth in due time. George carried with him a very vivid recollection of his vision on the return voyage, and never doubted for an instant that his brother had been actually murdered in the manner and by the persons named, as seen in the vision. He carried with him the determination to bring the villains to justice and was filled with the conviction that through his efforts retribution would fall upon the murderers.

In England, justice was at work—but the missing link was needed. The crime aroused universal horror and indignation, and the authorities left nothing undone in the direction of discovering the murderers and bringing them to justice. Two brothers named Hightwood were suspected, and in their cottage were found blood-stained garments. But no pistol was found, although the younger brother admitted having owned but lost one. They were arrested and brought before the magistrates. The evidence against them was purely circumstantial, and not any too strong at that; but their actions were those of guilty men. They were committed for trial. Each confessed, in hopes of saving his life and obtaining imprisonment instead. But both were convicted and sentenced to be hanged. There was doubt in the minds of some, however, about the pistol. The story continues:

"Before the execution, George Northey arrived from St. Helena, and declared that the pistol was in the thatch of the old cottage close by the place where they had murdered Hart Northey, and where they had hid it. 'How do you know?' he was asked. George replied: 'I saw the foul deed committed in a dream I had the night of the murder, when at St. Helena.' The pistol was found, as George Northey had predicted, in the thatch of the ruined cottage." Investigation revealed that the details of the crime were identical with those seen in the vision.

It is a fact known to all occultists that many persons frequently travel in the astral body during sleep; and in many cases retain a faint recollection of some of the things they have seen and heard during their travels in the astral. Nearly everyone knows the experience of waking up in the morning feeling physically tired and "used up;" in some cases a dim recollection of walking or working during the dream being had. Who among us has not had the experience of "walking on the air," or in the air, without the feet touching the ground, being propelled simply by the effort of the will? And who of us has had not experienced that dreadful—"falling through space" sensation, in dreams, with the sudden awakening just before we actually struck earth? And who has not had the mortifying dream experience of walking along the street, or in some public place, and being suddenly overcome by the consciousness that we were in our night-clothes, or perhaps without any clothing at all? All of these things are more or less distorted recollection of astral journeyings.

But while these dream excursions in the astral are harmless, the conscious "going out in the astral" is not so. There are many planes of the astral into which it is dangerous and unpleasant for the uninstructed person to travel; unless accompanied by a capable occultist as guide. Therefore, I caution all students against trying to force development in that direction. Nature surrounds you with safeguards, and interposes obstacles for your own protection and good. Do not try to break through these obstacles without knowledge of what you are doing. "Fools rush in where angels fear to tread," remember; and "a little learning is a dangerous thing." When you have reached the stage of development in which it will be safe for you to undertake conscious astral explorations, then will your guide be at hand, and the instruction furnished you by those capable of giving it to you. Do not try to break into the astral without due preparation, and full knowledge, lest you find yourself in the state of the fish who leaped out of the water onto the banks of the stream. Your dream trips are safe; they will increase in variety and clearness, and you will remember more about them—all this before you may begin to try to consciously "go out into the astral" as do the occultists. Be content to crawl before you may walk. Learn to add, multiply, subtract and divide, before you undertake the higher mathematics, algebra, geometry, etc., of occultism.

LESSON - XV

STRANGE ASTRAL PHENOMENA

There are several phases of astral phenomena other than those mentioned in the preceding chapters, which it will be better for the student to become acquainted with in order to round out his general knowledge of the subject, although the manifestations are comparatively rare, and not so generally recognized in works on this subject.

One of the first of these several phases of astral phenomena is that which may be called Thought-Form Projection. This manifestation comes in the place on the psychic scale just between ordinary clairvoyance on the one hand, and astral body projection on the other. It has some of the characteristics of each, and is often mistaken for one or the other of these phases.

To understand this phenomena, the student should know something regarding the fact that thought frequently takes on astral form, and that these manifestations are known as thought-forms. I have spoken of these in some of the preceding lessons. The ordinary thought-form is quite simple, as a rule, and does not bear any particular resemblance to the sender thereof. But in some cases a person may, consciously or unconsciously, strongly and clearly think of himself as present at some other place, and thus actually create a thought-form of himself at that place, which may be discerned by those having clairvoyant vision. Moreover, this thought-form of himself is connected psychically with himself and affords a channel of psychic information for him. As a rule these thought-forms are only projected by those who have trained their minds and will along occult lines; but occasionally under the stress of strong emotion or desire an ordinary person may focus his psychic power to such an extent that the phenomena is manifested.

Here I will quote from an English investigator of astral phenomena, who has had much experience on that plane. He says: "All students are aware that thought takes form, at any rate upon its own plane, and in the majority of cases upon the astral plane also; but it may not be so generally known that if a man thinks strongly of himself as present at any given place, the form assumed by that particular thought will be a likeness of the thinker himself, which will appear at the place in question. Essentially this form must be composed of the matter of the mental plane, but in very many cases it would draw round itself matter of the astral plane also, and so would approach much nearer to visibility. There are, in fact, many instances in which it has been seen by the person thought of—most probably by means of the unconscious influence emanating from the original thinker. None of the consciousness of the thinker would, however, be included within this thought-form. When once sent out from him, it would normally be a quite separate entity—not indeed absolutely unconnected with its maker, but practically so as far as the possibility of receiving any impression through it is concerned.

"This type of clairvoyance consists, then, in the power to retain so much connection with and so much hold over a newly-created thought-form as will render it possible to receive impressions by means of it. Such impressions as were made upon the form would in this case be transmitted to the thinker—not along an astral telegraph line, but by a sympathetic vibration. In a perfect case of this kind of clairvoyance it is almost as though the seer projected a part of his consciousness into the thought-form, and used it as a kind of outpost, from which observation was possible. He sees almost as well as he would if he himself stood in the place of his thought-form. The figures at which he is looking will appear to him as of life-size and close to hand, instead of tiny and at a distance as in the case of some other forms of clairvoyance; and he will find it possible to shift his point of view if he wishes to do so. Clairaudience is perhaps less frequently associated with this type of clairvoyance than with the others, but its place is to some extent taken by a kind of mental perception of the thoughts and intentions of those who are seen.

"Since the man's consciousness is still in the physical body, he will be able (even when exercising this faculty) to hear and to speak, in so far as he can do this without any distraction of his attention. The moment that the intentness of his thought fails, the whole vision is gone, and he will have to construct a fresh thought-form before he can resume it. Instances in which this kind of sight is possessed with any degree of perfection by untrained people are naturally rarer than in the other types of clairvoyance, because the capacity for mental control required, and the generally finer nature of the forces employed."

I may mention that this particular method is frequently employed by advanced occultists of all countries, being preferred for various reasons. Some of the reasons of this preference as follows: (a) The ability to shift the vision, and to turn around almost as well as in the case of actual astral-body projection—this gives quite an advantage to this method over the method of ordinary clairvoyance; (b) it does away with certain disadvantages of "going out into the astral" in the astral-body, which only trained occultists realize—

it gives almost the same results as astral-body clairvoyance, without a number of disadvantages and inconveniences.

In India, especially, this form of clairvoyance is comparatively frequent. This by reason of the fact that the Hindus, as a race, are far more psychic than are those of the Western lands, all else considered; and, besides, there are a much greater number of highly developed occultists there than in the West. Moreover, there is a certain psychic atmosphere surrounding India, by reason of its thousands of years of deep interest in things psychic and spiritual, all of which renders the production of psychic phenomena far easier than in other lands.

In India, moreover, we find many instances of another form of psychic, or astral phenomena. I allude to the production of thought-form pictures which are plainly visible to one or more persons. This phase of psychic phenomena is the real basis for many of the wonder tales which Western travellers bring back with them from India. The wonderful cases of magical appearance of living creatures and plants, and other objects, out of the clear air are the result of this psychic phenomena. That is to say, the creatures and objects are not really produced—they are but astral appearances resulting from the projection of powerful thought-forms from the mind of the magician or other wonder-worker, of whom India has a plentiful supply. Even the ignorant fakirs (I use the word in its true sense, not in the sense given it by American slang)—even these itinerant showmen of psychic phenomena, are able to produce phenomena of this kind which seems miraculous to those witnessing them. As for the trained occultists of India, I may say that their feats (when they deign to produce them) seem to overturn every theory and principle of materialistic philosophy and science. But in nearly every case the explanation is the same—the projection of a strong and clear thought-form on a large scale.

Although I have purposely omitted reference to Hindu psychic phenomena in this book (for the reason given in my Introduction), I find it necessary to quote cases in India in this connection, for the simple reason that there are but few counterparts in the Western world. There are no itinerent wonder-workers of this kind in Western lands, and the trained occultists of the West of course would not consent to perform feats of this kind for the amusement of persons seeking merely sensations. The trained wills of the West are given rather to materializing objectively on the physical plane, creating great railroads, buildings, bridges, etc., from the mental pictures, rather than devoting the same time, energy and will to the production of astral though-forms and pictures. There is a great difference in temperament, as well as a difference in the general psychic atmosphere, between East and West, which serves to explain matters of this kind.

An American writer truly says: "The first principle underlying the whole business of Hindu wonder-working is that of a strong will; and the first necessary condition of producing a magical effect is an increase in the power of thought. The Hindus, owing to that intense love for solitary meditation, which has been one of the most pronounced characteristics from time immemorial, have acquired mental faculties of which we of the Western and younger civilization are totally ignorant. The Hindu has attained a past master's degree in speculative philosophy. He has for years retired for meditation to the silent places in his land, lived a hermit, subdued the body and developed the mind, thus winning control over other minds."

In India, I have seen scenes of far distant places appearing as a mirage in clear air, even the colors being present to the scenes. This, though some what uncommon, was simply a remarkable instance of thought-form projection from the mind of a man highly developed along occult lines. You must remember that in order to produce a picture in the astral, of this kind, the occultist must not only have the power of will and mind to cause such a picture to materialize, but he must also have a remarkable memory for detail in the picture—for nothing appears in the picture unless it has already been pictured in the mind of the mind of the man himself. Such a memory and perception of detail is very rare—in the Western world it is possessed by only exceptional artists; however, anyone may cultivate this perception and memory if he will give the time and care to it that the Hindu magicians do.

You have heard of the Hindu Mango Trick, in which the magician takes a mango seed, plants it in the ground, waves his hands over it, and then causes first a tiny shoot to appear from the surface of the ground, this followed by a tiny trunk, and leaves, which grow and grow, until at last appears a full sized mango tree, which first shows blossoms and then ripe fruit. In short, in a few moments the magician has produced that which Nature require years to do—that is he apparently does this. What he really does is to produce a wonderful thought-form in the astral, from seed stage to tree and fruit stage; the astral picture reproducing perfectly the picture in his own mind. It is as if he were creating a moving picture film-roll in his mind, and then projecting this upon the screen of the air. There is no mango tree there, and never was, outside of the mind of the magician and the minds of his audience.

In the same way, the magician will seem to throw the end of a rope up into the air. It travels far up until the end is lost sight of. Then he sends a boy climbing up after it, until he too disappears from sight. Then he causes the whole thing to disappear, and lo! the boy is seen standing among the audience. The boy is real, of course, but he never left the spot—the rest was all an appearance caused by the mind and will of the magician, pictured in the astral as a thought-form. In the same way the magician will seem to cut the boy into bits, and then cause the severed parts to spring together and reassemble themselves. These feats may be varied indefinitely but the principle is ever the same—thought-form projection.

Western visitors have sought to obtain photographs of these feats of the Hindu magicians, but their plates and films invariably show nothing whatever except the old fakir sitting quietly in the centre, with a peculiar expression in his eyes. This is as might be expected, for the picture exists only in the astral, and is perceived only by the awakened astral senses of those present, which have been stimulated into activity by the power of the magician—by sympathetic vibration, to be exact. Moreover, in certain instances it has been found that the vision is confined to a limited area; persons outside of the limit-ring see nothing, and those moving nearer to the magician lose sight of what they had previously seen. There are scientific reasons for this last fact, which need not be gone into at this place. The main point I am seeking to bring out is that these wonderful scenes are simply and wholly thought-form pictures in the astral, perceived by the awakened astral vision of those present. This to be sure is wonderful enough—but still no miracle has been worked!

I may mention here that these magicians begin their training from early youth. In addition to certain instruction concerning astral phenomena which is handed down from father to son among them they are set to work practicing "visualization" of things previously perceived. They are set to work upon, say, a rose. They must impress upon their memory the perfect picture of the rose—no easy matter, I may tell you. Then they proceed to more difficult objects, slowly and gradually, along well known principles of memory development. Along with this they practice the art of reproducing that which they remember—projecting it in thought-form state. And so the young magician proceeds, from simple to complex things; from easy to difficult; until, finally, he is pronounced fit to give public exhibitions. All this takes years and years—sometimes the boy grows to be a middle-aged man before he is allowed to publicly exhibit his power. Imagine a Western boy or man being willing to study from early childhood to middle-age before he may hope to be able to show what he has been learning! Verily "the East is East, and the West is West"—the two poles of human activity and expression.

Another phase of psychic astral phenomena which should be mentioned, although it is manifested but comparatively seldom, is that which has been called "Telekinesis." By the term "telekinesis" is meant that class of phenomena which manifests in the movement of physical objects without physical contact with the person responsible for the movement. I understand that the term itself was coined by Professor Cowes, with whose works I am not personally familiar. It is derived from the two Greek words TELE, meaning "far off," and KINESIS, meaning "to move."

This class of phenomena is known better in the Western world by reason of its manifestation in spiritualistic circles in the movement of tables, etc.; the knocking or tapping on tables and doors, etc.; all of which are usually attributed to the work of "spirits," but which occultists know are generally produced, consciously or unconsciously, by means of the power in the medium or others present, sometimes both. I would say here that I am not trying to discredit genuine spiritualistic phenomena—I am not considering the same in these lessons. All that I wish to say is that many of the phenomena commonly attributed to "spirits" are really but results of the psychic forces inherent in the living human being.

Under certain conditions there may appear in the case of a person strongly psychic, and also strongly charged with prana, the ability to extend a portion of the astral body to a considerable distance, and to there produce an effect upon some physical object. Those with strong clairvoyant vision may actually perceive this astral extension, under favorable circumstances. They perceive the astral arm of the person stretching out, diminishing in size as it extends (just as a piece of flexible rubber shrinks in diameter as it expands in length) and finally coming in contact with the physical object it wishes to move or strike. Then is seen a strong flow of prana along its length, which (by a peculiar form of concentration) is able to produce the physical effect. I cannot enter into the subject of astral physics at this place, for the subject is far too technical to be treated in lessons designed for general study. I may at least partially explain the phenomenon, however, by saying that the projected astral arm acts in a manner almost precisely like that of an extended physical arm, were such a thing possible in nature.

This astral-body extension produces spirit raps on tables; table-tilting and movement; levitation, or the lifting of solid objects in the air; playing upon musical instruments such as the guitar, accordian, etc. In some cases it is able to actually lift the person himself from the floor, and carry him through the air, in the same way. It may also cause the movement of a pencil in a closed slate, or bit of chalk upon a blackboard. In fact, it may produce almost any form of movement possible to the physical hand. In the case of the levitation of the person himself, the astral arms, and sometimes the legs as well, extend to the floor and push up the physical body into the air, and then propel it along. There are many complex technical details to these manifestations, however, and in a general statement these must be omitted.

Some who are firmly wedded to the spiritistic theory resent the statement of occultists that this form of phenomena may be explained without the necessity of the "spirits." But the best ground for the statement of the occultists is that many advanced occultists are able to produce such phenomena, consciously, by an act of pure will, accompanied by the power of mental picturing. They first picture the astral extension, and then will the projection of the astral and the passage of the prana (or vital force) around the pattern of the mental image. In the case of some very highly developed occultists the astral thought-form of their body becomes so charged with prana that it is able to move physical objects. There are not mere theories, for they may be verified by any occultist of sufficiently high development.

I do not wish to intimate that the mediums are aware of the true nature of this phenomena, and consciously deceive their followers. On the contrary, most of them firmly believe that it is the "spirits" who do the work; unaware that they are unconsciously projecting their astral bodies, charged with prana, and performing the feat themselves. The best mediums, however, will generally tell you that they strongly "wish" that the thing be done, and a little cross-examination will reveal the fact that they generally make a clear mental picture of the actual happening just before it occurs. As I have already stated, however, the best proof is the fact that advanced occultists are able to duplicate the phenomena deliberately, consciously, and at will. I do not think that detracts from the wonder and interest in the so-called "spiritistic" phenomena; on the contrary, I think that it adds to it.

Again invading the realm of the "spirits," I would say that occultists know that many cases of so-called materialization of "spirit-forms" take place by reason of the unconscious projection of the astral body of the medium. Moreover, such a projection of the astral body may take on the appearance of some departed soul, by reason of the mental picture of that person in the mind of the medium. But, it may be asked if the medium has never seen the dead person, how can he or she make a mental picture of him or her. The answer is that the minds of the persons present who knew the dead person tend to influence the appearance of the nebulous spirit form. In fact, in most cases the medium is unable to produce the phenomenon without the psychic assistance of those in the circle. In this case, also, I would say that the advanced occultist is able to duplicate the phenomena at will, as all who have enjoyed the privilege of close acquaintance with such persons are aware.

The fact the medium is usually in a trance condition aid materially in the ease with which the phenomena are produced. With the conscious mind stilled, and the subconscious mind active, the astral phenomena are produced with much less trouble than would be the case if the medium were in the ordinary condition.

Now, I wish to impress upon the minds of those of my readers who have a strong sympathy for the spiritistic teachings that I recognize the validity and genuineness of much of the phenomena of spiritism—I know these things to be true, for that matter; it is not a matter of mere belief on my part. But I also know that much of the so-called spiritistic phenomena is possible without the aid of "spirits," but by, the employment of the psychic astral forces and powers as stated in these lessons. I see no reason for any honest investigator of spiritism to be offended at such statements, for it does not take away from the wonder of the phenomena; and does not discredit the motives and power of the mediums. We must search for truth wherever it is to be found; and we must not seek to dodge the results of our investigations. There is too much wonderful phenomena in spiritism to begrudge the explanation that the occultist offers for certain of its phases.

While I am on the subject of materialization however, I would direct the attention of the student to my little book entitled "The Astral World," in which I have explained briefly the phenomena of those planes of the astral in which dwell the cast-off shells of souls which have moved on to the higher planes of the great astral world. I have there shown that many astral shells or shades, or other astral semi-entities may be materialized, and thus mistaken for the "spirits" of departed friends. I have also explained in the same little book how there are certain powerful thought-forms which may be mistaken for spirit materializations. I have also shown how many a honest medium is really a good clairvoyant, and by reading the records of the astral light is able to give information which seems to come from the departed soul. All of these things should be familiar to the earnest investigator of spiritism, in order that he may be able to classify the phenomena which he witnesses, and to avoid error and disappointment.

In this connection, before passing on to the consideration of other phases of psychic phenomena, I would say that one of the best mediums known to the modern Western world—a medium who has been consulted by eminent men, university professors, psychologists, and others—and whose revelations regarding past, present and future astounded careful and intelligent men of international reputation—this medium at the height of her professional success made a public announcement that she felt compelled, from conscientious motives, to assert that she had come to the conclusion that her message came not from departed "spirits" but rather from some unknown realm of being, brought hither by the exercise of some faculty inherent in her and developed to a high power in her for some reason, which power seem to manifest more effectively when she shut off her ordinary physical faculties and functioned on a plane higher than them. I think that the student of the present lessons will be able to point out the nature of the phenomena manifested by this medium, and also the source of her power. If not, I shall feel disappointed at my work of instruction.

LESSON - XVI

PSYCHIC INFLUENCE; ITS LAWS AND PRINCIPLES

One of the phases of psychic phenomena that actively engage the attention of the student from the very beginning is that which may be called Psychic Influence. By this term is meant the influencing of one mind by another—the effect of one mind over another. There has been much written and said on this phase of the general subject in recent years, but few writers, however, have gone deeply into the matter.

In the first place, most of the writers on the subject seek to explain the whole thing by means of ordinary telepathy. But this is merely a one-sided view of the truth of the matter. For, while ordinary telepathy plays an important part in the phenomena, still the higher form of telepathy, i.e., astral thought-transference, is frequently involved. The student who has followed me in the preceding lessons will understand readily what I mean when I say this, so there is no necessity for repetition on this point at this place.

At this point, however, I must ask the student to consider the idea of psychic vibrations and their inductive power. It is a great principle of occultism, as well as of modern science, that everything is in a state of vibration—everything has its own rate of vibration, and is constantly manifesting it. Every mental state is accompanied by vibration of its own plane: every emotional state or feeling has its own particular rate of vibration. These rates of vibrations manifest just as do the vibrations of musical sound which produce the several notes on the scale, one rising above the other in rate of vibration. But the scale of mental and emotional states is far more complex, and far more extended than is the musical scale; there are thousands of different notes, and half-notes, on the mental scale. There are harmonies and discords on that scale, also.

To those to whom vibrations seem to be something merely connected with sound-waves, etc., I would say that a general and hasty glance at some elementary work on physical science will show that even the different shades, hues and tints of the colors perceived by us arise from different rates of vibrations. Color is nothing more than the result of certain rates of vibrations of light recorded by our senses and interpreted by our minds. From the low vibrations of red to the high vibrations of violet, all the various colors of the spectrum have their own particular rate of vibration. And, more than this, science knows that below the lowest red vibrations, and above the highest violet vibrations, there are other vibrations which our senses are unable to record, but which scientific instruments register. The rays of light by which photographs are taken are not perceived by the eye. There are a number of so-called chemical rays of light which the eye does not perceive, but which may be caught by delicate instruments. There is what science has called "dark light," which will photograph in a room which appears pitch dark to the human sight.

Above the ordinary scale of light vibrations are the vibrations of the X-Rays and other fine forces—these are not perceived by the eye, but are caught by delicate instruments and recorded. Moreover, though science has not as yet discovered the fact, occultists know that the vibrations of mental and emotional states are just as true and regular as are those of sound or light, or heat. Again, above the plane of the physical vibrations arising from the brain and nervous system, there are the vibrations of the astral counterparts of these, which are much higher in the scale. For even the astral faculties and organs, while above the physical, still are under the universal rule of vibration, and have their own rate thereof. The old occult axiom: "As above, so below; as below, so above" is always seen to work out on all planes of universal energy.

Closely following this idea of the universality of vibrations, and intimately connected therewith, we have the principle of "induction," which is likewise universal, and found manifesting on all planes of energy. "What is induction?" you may ask. Well, it is very simple, or very complex—just as you may look at it. The principle of induction (on any plane) is that inherent quality or attribute of energy by which the manifestation of energy tends to reproduce itself in a second object, by setting up corresponding vibrations therein, though without direct contact of the two objects.

Thus, heat in one object tends to induce heat in another object within its range of induction—the heated object "throws off" heat vibrations which set up corresponding vibrations in the near-by second object and make it hot. Likewise, the vibrations of light striking upon other objects render them capable of radiating light. Again, a magnet will induce magnetism in a piece of steel suspended nearby, though the two objects do not actually touch, each other. An object which is electrified will by induction electrify another object situated some distance away. A note sounded on the piano, or violin, will cause a glass or vase in some distant part of the room to vibrate and "sing," under certain conditions. And, so on, in every form or phase of the manifestation of energy do we see the principle of induction in full operation and manifestation.

On the plane of ordinary thought and emotion, we find many instances of this principle of induction. We know that one person vibrating strongly with happiness or sorrow, cheerfulness or anger, as the case may be fends to communicate his feeling and emotions, state to those with whom he comes in contact. All of you have seen a whole room full of persons affected and influenced in this way, under certain circumstances. You have also seen how a magnetic orator, preacher, singer or actor is able to induce in his audience a state of emotional vibration corresponding to that manifested by himself. In the same manner the "mental atmospheres" of towns, cities, etc., are induced.

A well-known writer on this subject has truthfully told us: "We all know how great waves of feeling spread over a town, city or country, sweeping people off their balance. Great waves of political enthusiasm, or war-spirit, or prejudice for or against certain persons, sweep over places and cause men to act in a manner that they will afterward regret when they come to themselves and consider their acts in cold blood. They will be swayed by demagogues or magnetic leaders who wish to gain their votes or patronage; and they will be led into acts of mob violence, or similar atrocities, by yielding to these waves of contagious thought. On the other hand, we all know how great waves of religious feeling sweep over a community upon the occasion of some great 'revival' excitement or fervor."

These things being perceived, and recognized as true, the next question that presents itself to the mind of the intelligent student is this: "But what causes the difference in power and effect between the thought and feeling-vibrations of different persons?" This question is a valid one, and arises from a perception of the underlying variety and difference in the thought vibrations of different persons. The difference, my students, is caused by three principal facts, viz., (1) difference in degree of feeling; (2) difference in degree of visualization; and (3) difference in degree of concentration. Let us examine each of these successively, so as to get at the underlying principle.

The element of emotional feeling is like the element of fire in the production of steam. The more vivid and intense the feeling or emotion, the greater the degree of heat and force to the thought wave or vibratory stream projected. You will begin to see why the thought vibrations of those animated and filled with strong desire, strong wish, strong ambition, etc., must be more forceful than those of persons of the opposite type.

The person who is filled with a strong desire, wish or ambition, which has been fanned into a fierce blaze by attention, is a dynamic power among other persons, and his influence is felt. In fact, it may be asserted that as a general rule no person is able to influence men and things unless he have a strong desire, wish or ambition within him. The power of desire is a wonderful one, as all occultists know, and it will accomplish much even if the other elements be lacking; while, in proper combination with other principles it will accomplish wonders. Likewise, a strong interest in a thing will cause a certain strength to the thought-vibrations connected therewith. Interest is really an emotional feeling, though we generally think of it as merely something connected with the intellect. A cold intellectual thought has very little force, unless backed up by strong interest and concentration. But any intellectual thought backed up with interest, and focused by concentration, will produce very strong thought vibrations, with a marked inductive power.

Now, let us consider the subject of visualization. Every person knows that the person who wishes to accomplish anything, or who expects to do good work along any line, must first know what he wishes to accomplish. In the degree that he is able to see the thing in his mind's eye—to picture the thing in his imagination—in that degree will he tend to manifest the thing itself in material form and effect.

Sir Francis Galton, an eminent authority upon psychology, says on this point: "The free use of a high visualizing faculty is of much importance in connection with the higher processes of generalized thought. A visual image is the most perfect form of mental representation wherever the shape, position, and relations of objects to space are concerned. The best workmen are those who visualize the whole of what they propose to do before they take a tool in their hands. Strategists, artists of all denominations, physicists who contrive new experiments, and, in short, all who do not follow routine, have need of it. A faculty that is of importance in all technical and artistic occupations, that gives accuracy to our perceptions and justice to our generalizations, is starved by lazy disuse instead of being cultivated judiciously in such a way as will, on the whole, bring best return. I believe that a serious study of the best way of developing and utilizing this faculty, without prejudice to the practice of abstract thought in symbols, is one of the pressing desirata in the yet unformed science of education."

Not only on the ordinary planes is the forming of strong mental images important and useful, but when we come to consider the phenomena of the astral plane we begin to see what an important part is played there by strong mental images or visualized ideas. The better you know what you desire, wish or aspire to, the stronger will be your thought vibrations of that thing, of course. Well, then, the stronger that you are able to picture the thing in your mind—to visualize it to yourself—the stronger will be your actual knowledge and thought-form of that thing. Instead of your thought vibrations being grouped in nebulous forms, lacking shape and distinct figure, as in the ordinary case; when you form strong, clear mental images of what you desire or wish to accomplish, then do the thought vibrations group themselves in clear, strong distinct forms. This being done, when the mind of other persons are affected by induction they get the clear idea of the thought and feeling in your mind, and are strongly influenced thereby.

A little later on, I shall call your attention to the Attractive Power of Thought. But at this point I wish to say to you that while thought certainly attracts to you the things that you think of the most, still the power of the attraction depends very materially upon the clearness and distinctness of the mental image, or thought visualization, of the desired thing that you have set up in your mind. The nearer you can actually see the thing as you wish it to happen, even to the general details, the stronger will be the attractive force thereof. But, I shall leave the discussion of this phase of the subject until I reach it in its proper order. For the present, I shall content myself with urging upon you the importance of a clear mental image, or visualized thought, in the matter of giving force and direction to the idea induced in the minds of other persons. In order for the other persons to actually perceive clearly the idea or feeling induced in them, it is necessary that the idea or feeling be strongly visualized in the mind originating it; that is the whole thing in one sentence.

The next point of importance in thought-influence by induction, is that which is concerned with the process of concentration. Concentration is the act of mental focusing, or bringing to a single point or centre. It is like the work of the sun-glass that converges the rays of the sun to a single tiny point, thus immensely increasing its heat and power. Or, it is like the fine point of a needle that will force its way through where a blunt thing cannot penetrate. Or, it is like the strongly concentrated essence of a chemical substance, of which one drop is as powerful as one pint of the original thing. Think of the concentrated power of a tiny drop of attar of roses—it has within its tiny space the concentrated odor of thousands of roses; one drop of it will make a pint of extract, and a gallon of weaker perfumery! Think of the concentrated power in a lightning flash, as contrasted with the same amount of electricity diffused over a large area. Or, think of the harmless flash of a small amount of gunpowder ignited in the open air, as contrasted with the ignition of the same amount of powder compelled to escape through the small opening in the gun-barrel.

The occult teachings lay great stress upon this power of mental concentration. All students of the occult devote much time and care to the cultivation of the powers of concentration, and the development of the ability to employ them. The average person possesses but a very small amount of concentration, and is able to concentrate his mind for but a few moments at a time. The trained thinker obtains much of his mental power from his acquired ability to concentrate on his task. The occultist trains himself in fixing his concentrated attention upon the matter before him, so as to bring to a focal centre all of his mental forces.

The mind is a very restless thing, and is inclined to dance from one thing to another, tiring of each thing after a few moment's consideration thereof. The average person allows his involuntary attention to rest upon every trifling thing, and to be distracted by the idlest appeals to the senses. He finds it most difficult to either shut out these distracting appeals to the senses, and equally hard to hold the attention to some uninteresting thing. His attention is almost free of control by the will, and the person is a slave to his perceptive powers and to his imagination, instead of, being a master of both.

The occultist, on the contrary, masters his attention, and controls his imagination. He forces the one to concentrate when he wishes it to do so; and he compels the latter to form the mental images he wishes to visualize. But this a far different thing from the self-hypnotization which some persons imagine to be concentration. A writer on the subject has well said: "The trained occultist will concentrate upon a subject or object with a wonderful intensity, seemingly completely absorbed in the subject or object before him, and oblivious to all else in the world. And yet, the task accomplished, or the given time expired, he will detach his mind from the object and will be perfectly fresh, watchful and wide-awake to the next matter before him. There is every difference between being controlled by involuntary attention, which is species of self-hypnotization, and the control of the attention, which is an evidence of mastery." An eminent French psychologist once said: "The authority of the attention is subject to the superior authority of the Ego. I yield it, or I withhold it, as I please. I direct it in turn to several points. I concentrate it upon each point, as long as my will can stand the effort."

In an earlier lesson of this series, I have indicated in a general way the methods whereby one may develop and train his powers of concentration. There is no royal road to concentration; it may be developed only by practice and exercise. The secret consists in managing the attention, so as to fix it upon a subject, no matter how uninteresting; and to hold it there for a reasonable length of time. Practice upon some disagreeable study or other task is good exercise, for it serves to train the will in spite of the influence of more attractive objects or subjects. And this all serves to train the will, remember; for the will is actively concerned in every act of voluntary attention. In fact, attention of this kind is one of the most important and characteristic acts of the will.

So, as you see, in order to be successful in influencing the minds of others by means of mental induction, you must first cultivate a strong feeling of interest in the idea which you wish to induce in the other person, or a strong desire to produce the thing. Interest and desire constitute the fire which generates the stream of will from the water of mind, as some occultists have stated it. Secondly, you must cultivate the faculty of forming strong and clear mental images of the idea or feeling you wish to so induce; you must learn to actually "see" the thing in your imagination, so as to give the idea strength and clearness. Thirdly, you must learn to concentrate your mind and attention upon the idea or feeling, shutting out all other ideas and feelings for the time being; thus you give concentrated force and power to the vibrations and thought-forms which you are projecting.

These three principles underlie all of the many forms of mental induction, or mental influence. We find them in active operation in cases in which the person is seeking to attract to himself certain conditions, environment, persons, things, or channels of expression, by setting into motion the great laws of mental attraction. We see them also employed when the person is endeavoring to produce an effect upon the mind of some particular person, or number of persons. We see them in force in all cases of mental or psychic healing, under whatever form it may be employed. In short, these are general principles, and must therefore underlie all forms and phases of mental or psychic influence. The sooner the student realizes this fact, and the more actively does he set himself to work in cultivating and developing these principles within himself, the more successful and efficient will he become in this field of psychic research and investigation. It is largely in the degree of the cultivation of these three mental principles that the occultist is distinguished from the ordinary man.

It may be that you are not desirous of cultivating or practicing the power of influencing other persons psychically. Well, that is for you to decide for yourself. At any rate, you will do well to develop yourselves along these lines, at least for self-protection. The cultivation of these three mental principles will tend to make you active and positive, psychically, as contrasted with the passive, negative mental state of the average person. By becoming mentally active and positive you will be able to resist any psychic influence that may be directed toward yourself, and to surround yourself with a protective aura of positive, active mental vibrations.

And, moreover, if you are desirous of pursuing your investigations of psychic and astral phenomena, you will find it of great importance to cultivate and develop these three principles in your mind. For, then you will be able to brush aside all distracting influences, and to proceed at once to the task before you, with power, clearness and strength of purpose and method.

In the following chapters I shall give you a more or less detailed presentation of the various phases or forms of psychic influence. Some of these may seem at first to be something independent of the general principles. But I ask that you carefully analyze all of these, so as to discover that the same fundamental principles are under and back of each and every instance presented. When you once fully grasp this fact, and perfect yourselves in the few fundamental principles, then you are well started on the road to mastery of all the various phases of psychic phenomena. Instead of puzzling your mind over a hundred different phases of disconnected phenomena, it is better to master the few actual elementary principles, and then reason deductively from these to the various manifestation thereof. Master the principles, and then learn to apply them.

LESSON - XVII

PERSONAL PSYCHIC INFLUENCE OVER OTHERS

Psychic Influence, as the term is used in this book, may be said to be divided into three general classes, viz., (1) Personal Influence, in which the mind of another is directly influenced by induction while he is in the presence of the person influencing; (2) Distant Influencing, in which the psychic induction is directly manifested when the persons concerned are distant from one another; and (3) Indirect Influence, in which the induction is manifested in the minds of various persons coming in contact with the thought vibrations of the person manifesting them, though no attempt is made to directly influence any particular person. I shall now present each of these three forms of psychic influence to you for consideration, one after the other in the above order.

Personal Influence, as above defined, ranges from cases in which the strongest control (generally known as hypnotism) is manifested, down to the cases in which merely a slight influence is exerted. But the general principle underlying all of these cases is precisely the same. The great characters of history, such as Alexander the Great, Napoleon Bonaparte, and Julius Caesar, manifested this power to a great degree, and were able to sway men according to their will. All great leaders of men have this power strongly manifested, else they would not be able to influence the minds of men. Great orators, preachers, statesmen, and others of this class, likewise manifest the power strongly. In fact, the very sign of ability to influence and manage other persons is evidence of the possession and manifestation of this mighty power.

In developing this power to influence others directly and personally, you should begin by impressing upon your mind the principles stated in the preceding chapter, namely (1) Strong Desire; (2) Clear Visualization; and (3) Concentration.

You must begin by encouraging a strong desire in your mind to be a positive individual; to exert and manifest a positive influence over others with whom you come in contact, and especially over those whom you wish to influence in some particular manner or direction. You must let the fire of desire burn fiercely within you, until it becomes as strong as physical hunger or thirst. You must "want to" as you want to breathe, to live. You will find that the men who accomplish the great things in life are those who have strong desire burning in their bosoms. There is a strong radiative and inductive power in strong desire and wish—in fact, some have thought this the main feature of what we generally call strong will-power.

The next step, of course, is the forming of a clear, positive, distinct and dynamic mental picture of the idea or feeling that you wish to induce in the other person. If it is an idea, you should make a strong clear picture of it in your imagination, so as to give it distinctness and force and a clear outline. If it is a feeling, you should picture it in your imagination. If it is something that you wish the other person to do, or some way in which you wish him to act, you should picture him as doing the thing, or acting in that particular way. By so doing you furnish the pattern or design for the induced mental or emotional states you wish to induce in the other person. Upon the clearness and strength of these mental patterns of the imagination depends largely the power of the induced impression.

The third step, of course, is the concentration of your mind upon the impression you wish to induce in the mind of the other person. You must learn to concentrate so forcibly and clearly that the idea will stand out clearly in your mind like a bright star of a dark night, except that there must be only one star instead of thousands. By so doing you really focus the entire force of your mental and psychic energies into that one particular idea or thought. This makes it act like the focused rays in the sun-glass, or like the strong pipe-stream of water that will break down the thing upon which it is turned. Diffused thought has but a comparatively weak effect, whereas a concentrated stream of thought vibrations will force its way through obstacles.

Remember, always, this threefold mental condition: (1) STRONG DESIRE; (2) CLEAR MENTAL PICTURE; and (3) CONCENTRATED THOUGHT. The greater the degree in which you can manifest these three mental conditions, the greater will be your success in any form of psychic influence, direct or indirect, personal or general, present or distant.

Before you proceed to develop the power to impress a particular idea or feeling upon the mind of another person, you should first acquire a positive mental atmosphere for yourself. This mental atmosphere is produced in precisely the same way that you induce a special idea or feeling in the mind of the other person. That is to say, you first strongly desire it, then you clearly picture it, and then you apply concentrated thought upon it.

I will assume that you are filled with the strong desire for a positive mental atmosphere around you. You want this very much indeed, and actually crave and hunger for it. Then you must begin to picture yourself (in your imagination) as surrounded with an aura of positive thought-vibrations which protect you from the thought forces of other persons, and, at the same time impress the strength of your personality upon the persons with whom you come in contact. You will be aided in making these strong mental pictures by holding the idea in your concentrated thought, and, at the same time, silently stating to your mind just what you expect to do in the desired direction. In stating your orders to your mind, always speak as if the thing were already accomplished at that particular moment. Never say that it "will be," but always hold fast to the "it is." The following will give you a good example of the mental statements, which of course should be accompanied by the concentrated idea of the thing, and the mental picture of yourself as being just what you state.

Here is the mental statement for the creation of a strong, positive psychic atmosphere: "I am surrounded by an aura of strong, positive, dynamic thought-vibrations. These render me positive to other persons, and render them negative to me. I am positive of their thought-vibrations, but they are negative to mine. They feel the strength of my psychic atmosphere, while I easily repel the power of theirs. I dominate the situation, and manifest my positive psychic qualities over theirs. My atmosphere creates the vibration of strength and power on all sides of me, which affect others with whom I come in contact. MY PSYCHIC ATMOSPHERE IS STRONG AND POSITIVE!"

The next step in Personal Influence is that of projecting your psychic power directly upon and into the mind of the other person whom you wish to influence. Sometimes, if the person is quite negative to you, this is a very simple and easy matter; but where the person is near your own degree of psychic positiveness you will have to assert your psychic superiority to him, and get the psychic "upper hand" before you can proceed further. This is accomplished by throwing into your psychic atmosphere some particularly strong mental statements accompanied by clear visualizations or mental pictures.

Make positive your psychic atmosphere, particularly towards the person whom you seek to influence, by statements and pictures something along the following lines: "I am positive to this man"; "He is negative to me"; "He feels my power and is beginning to yield to it"; "He is unable to influence me in the slightest, while I can influence him easily"; "My power is beginning to operate upon his mind and feelings." The exact words are not important, but the idea behind them gives them their psychic force and power.

Then should you begin your direct attack upon him, or rather upon his psychic powers. When I say "attack," I do not use the word in the sense of warfare or actual desire to harm the other person—this is a far different matter. What I mean to say is that there is usually a psychic battle for a longer or shorter period between two persons of similar degrees of psychic power and development. From this battle one always emerges victor at the time, and one always is beaten for the time being, at least. And, as in all battles, victory often goes to him who strikes the first hard blow. The offensive tactics are the best in cases of this kind.

A celebrated American author, Oliver Wendall Holmes, in one of his books makes mention of these duels of psychic force between individuals, as follows: "There is that deadly Indian hug in which men wrestle with their eyes, over in five seconds, but which breaks one of their two backs, and is good for three-score years and ten, one trial enough—settles the whole matter—just as when two feathered songsters of the barnyard, game and dunghill, come together. After a jump or two, and a few sharp kicks, there is an end to it; and it is 'After you, monsieur' with the beaten party in all the social relations for all the rest of his days."

An English physician, Dr. Fothergill by name, wrote a number of years ago about this struggle of wills, as he called it, but which is really a struggle of psychic power. He says: "The conflict of will, the power to command others, has been spoken of frequently. Yet what is this will-power that influences others? What is it that makes us accept, and adopt too, the advice of one person, while precisely the same advice from another has been rejected? Is it the weight of force of will which insensibly influences us; the force of will behind the advice? That is what it is! The person who thus forces his or her advice upon us has no more power to enforce it than others; but all the same we do as requested. We accept from one what we reject from another. One person says of something contemplated, 'Oh, but you must not,' yet we do it all the same, though that person may be in a position to make us regret the rejection of that counsel. Another person says, 'Oh, but you mustn't,' and we desist, though we may, if so disposed, set this latter person's opinion at defiance with impunity. It is not the fear of consequences, not of giving offense, which determines the adaption of the latter person's advice, while it has been rejected when given by the first. It depends upon the character or will-power of the individual advising whether we accept the advice or reject it. This character often depends little, if at all, in some cases, upon the intellect, or even upon the moral qualities, the goodness or badness, of the individual. It is itself an imponderable something; yet it carries weight with it. There may be abler men, cleverer men; but it is the one possessed of will who rises to the surface at these times—the one who can by some subtle power make other men obey him.

"The will-power goes on universally. In the young aristocrat who gets his tailor to make another advance in defiance of his conviction that he will never get his money back. It goes on between lawyer and client; betwixt doctor and patient; between banker and borrower; betwixt buyer and seller. It is not tact which enables the person behind the counter to induce customers to buy what they did not intend to buy, and which bought, gives them no satisfaction, though it is linked therewith for the effort to be successful. Whenever two persons meet in business, or in any other relation in life, up to love-making, there is this will-fight going on, commonly enough without any consciousness of the struggle. There is a dim consciousness of the result, but none of the processes. It often takes years of the intimacy of married life to find out with whom of the pair the mastery really lies. Often the far stronger character, to all appearances, has to yield; it is this will-element which underlies the statement: 'The race is not always to the swift, nor the battle to the strong.' In Middle-march' we find in Lydgate a grand aggregation of qualities, yet shallow, hard, selfish Rosamond masters him thoroughly in the end. He was not deficient in will-power; possessed more than an average amount of character; but in the fight he went down at last under the onslaught of the intense, stubborn will of his narrow-minded spouse. Their will-contest was the collision of a large warm nature, like a capable human hand, with a hard, narrow selfish nature, like a steel button; the hand only bruised itself while the button remained unaffected."

You must not, however, imagine that every person with whom you engage in one of these psychic duels is conscious of what is going on. He usually recognizes that some sort of conflict is under way, but he does not know the laws and principles of psychic force, and so is in the dark regarding the procedure. You will find that a little practice of this kind, in which no great question is involved, will give you a certain knack or trick of handling your psychic forces, and will, besides, give you that confidence in yourself that comes only from actual practice and exercise. I can point out the rules, and give you the principles, but you must learn the little bits of technique yourself from actual practice.

When you have crossed psychic swords with the other person, gaze at him intently but not fiercely, and send him this positive strong thought-vibration: "I am stronger than you, and I shall win!" At the same time picture to yourself your forces beating down his and overcoming him. Hold this idea and picture in your mind: "My vibrations are stronger than are yours—I am beating you!" Follow this up with the idea and picture of: "You are weakening and giving in—you are being overpowered!" A very powerful psychic weapon is the following: "My vibrations are scattering your forces—I am breaking your forces into bits—surrender, surrender now, I tell you!"

And now for some interesting and very valuable information concerning psychic defense. You will notice that in the offensive psychic weapons there is always an assertion of positive statement of your power and its effect. Well, then, in using the psychic defensive weapon against one of strong will or psychic force, you reverse the process. That is to say you deny the force of his psychic powers and forces, and picture them as melting into nothingness. Get this idea well fixed in your mind, for it is very important in a conflict of this kind. The effect of this is to neutralize all of the other person's power so far as its effect on yourself is concerned—you really do not destroy it in him totally. You simply render his forces powerless to affect you. This is important not only when in a psychic conflict of this kind, but also when you wish to render yourself immune from the psychic forces of other persons. You may shut yourself up in a strong defensive armor in this way, and others will be powerless to affect you.

In the positive statement, "I deny!" you have the Occult Shield of Defense, which is a mighty protection to you. Even if you do not feel disposed to cultivate and develop your psychic powers in the direction of influencing others, you should at least develop your defensive powers so as to resist any psychic attacks upon yourself.

You will find it helpful to practice these offensive and defensive weapons when you are alone, standing before your mirror and "playing" that your reflection in the glass is the other person. Send this imaginary other person the psychic vibrations, accompanied by the mental picture suitable for it. Act the part out seriously and earnestly, just as if the reflected image were really another person. This will give you confidence in yourself, and that indefinable "knack" of handling your psychic weapons that comes only from practice. You will do well to perfect yourself in these rehearsals, just as you would in case you were trying to master anything else. By frequent earnest rehearsals, you will gain not only familiarity with the process and methods, but you will also gain real power and strength by the exercise of your psychic faculties which have heretofore lain dormant. Just as you may develop the muscle of your arm by calisthenic exercises, until it is able to perform real muscular work of strength; so you may develop your psychic faculties in this rehearsal work, so that you will be strongly equipped and armed for an actual psychic conflict, besides having learned how to handle your psychic weapons.

After you have practiced sufficiently along the general offensive and defensive lines, and have learned how to manifest these forces in actual conflict, you will do well to practice special and specific commands to others, in the same way. That is to say, practice them first on your reflected image in the mirror. The following commands (with mental pictures, of course) will give you good practice. Go about the work in earnest, and act out the part seriously. Try these exercises: "Here! look at me!" "Give me your undivided attention!" "Come this way!" "Come to me at once!" "Go away from me—leave me at once!" "You like me—you like me very much!" "You are afraid of me!" "You wish to please me!" "You will agree to my proposition!" "You will do as I tell you!" Any special command you wish to convey to another person, psychically, you will do well to practice before the mirror in this way.

When you have made satisfactory progress in the exercises above mentioned, and are able, to demonstrate them with a fair degree of success in actual practice, you may proceed to experiment with persons along the lines of special and direct commands by psychic force. The following will give you a clear idea of the nature of the experiments in question, but you may enlarge upon and vary them indefinitely. Remember there is no virtue in mere words—the effect comes from the power of the thought behind the words. But, nevertheless, you will find that positive words, used in these silent commands, will help you to fit in your feeling to the words. Always make the command a real COMMAND, never a mere entreaty or appeal. Assume the mental attitude of a master of men—of a commander and ruler of other men. Here follow a number of interesting experiments along these lines, which will be very useful to you in acquiring the art of personal influence of this kind:

SEVEN VALUABLE EXERCISES

Exercise 1: When walking down the street behind a person, make him turn around in answer to your mental command. Select some person who does not seem to be too much rushed or too busy—select some person who seems to having nothing particular on his mind. Then desire earnestly that he shall turn around when you mentally call to him to do so; at the same time picture him as turning around in answer to your call; and at the same time concentrate your attention and thought firmly upon him. After a few moments of preparatory thought, send him the following message, silently of course, with as much force, positiveness and vigor as possible: "Hey there! turn around and look at me! Hey! turn around, turn around at once!" While influencing him fix your gaze at the point on his neck where the skull joins it—right at the base of the brain, in the back. In a number of cases, you will find that the person will look around as if someone had actually called him aloud. In other cases, he will seem puzzled, and will look from side to side as if seeking some one. After a little practice you will be surprised how many persons you can affect in this way.

Exercise 2: When in a public place, such as a church, concert or theatre, send a similar message to someone seated a little distance in front of you. Use the same methods as in the first exercise, and you will obtain similar results. It will seem queer to you at first to notice how the other person will begin to fidget and move around in his seat, and finally glance furtively around as if to see what is causing him the disturbance. You, of course, will not let him suspect that it is you, but, instead will gaze calmly ahead of you, and pretend not to notice him.

Exercise 3: This is a variation of the first exercise. It is practiced by sending to a person approaching you on the street, or walking ahead of you in the same direction, a command to turn to the right, or to the left, as you prefer. You will be surprised to see how often you will be successful in this.

Exercise 4: This is a variation of the second exercise. It is practiced by sending to a person seated in front of you in a public place the command to look to the right, or to the left, as you prefer. Do not practice on the same person too long, after succeeding at first—it is not right to torment people, remember.

Exercise 5: After having attained proficiency in the foregoing exercises, you many proceed to command a person to perform certain unimportant motions, such as rising or sitting down, taking off his hat, taking out his handkerchief, laying down a fan, umbrella, etc.

Exercise 6: The next step is to command persons to say some particular word having no important meaning; to "put words in his mouth" while talking to him. Wait until the other person pauses as if in search of a word, and then suddenly, sharply and forcibly put the word into his mouth, silently of course. In a very susceptible person, well under your psychic control, you may succeed in suggesting entire sentences and phrases to him.

Exercise 7: This is the summit of psychic influencing, and, of course, is the most difficult. But you will be surprised to see how well you will succeed in many cases, after you have acquired the knack and habit of sending the psychic message. It consists of commanding the person to obey the spoken command or request that you are about to make to him. This is the art and secret of the success of many salesmen, solicitors, and others working along the lines of influencing other people. It is acquired by beginning with small things, and gradually proceeding to greater, and still greater. At this point I should warn you that all the best occult teachings warn students against using this power for base ends, improper purposes, etc. Such practices tend to react and rebound against the person using them, like a boomerang. Beware against using psychic or occult forces for improper purposes—the psychic laws punish the offender, just as do the physical laws.

Finally, I caution the student against talking too much about his developing powers. Beware of boasting or bragging about these things. Keep silent, and keep your own counsel. When you make known your powers, you set into operation the adverse and antagonistic thought of persons around you who may be jealous of you, and who would wish to see you fail, or make yourself ridiculous. The wise head keepeth a still tongue! One of the oldest occult maxims is: "Learn! Dare! Do! Keep Silent!!!" You will do well to adhere strictly to this warning caution.

LESSON - XVIII

PSYCHIC INFLUENCE AT A DISTANCE

The second phase of Psychic Influence is that called Distant Psychic Influence, in which psychic induction is manifested when the persons are distant in space from one another—not in the presence of each other. Here, of course, we see the principle of telepathy involved in connection with the process of mental induction: and in some cases even the astral telepathic sense is called into operation.

The student who has followed my explanation and course of reasoning in the preceding lessons will readily perceive that the principle involved in this distant phase of psychic influence is precisely the same as that employed in direct personal psychic influence. As I have explained in an early lesson, it matters little whether the space to be covered by the psychic vibratory waves is but one foot or a thousand miles, the principle is exactly the same. There are, of course, other principles involved in the case of two persons meeting face to face and calling into force their psychic powers; for instance, there is the element of suggestion and association, and other psychological principles which are not in force when the two persons are out of the actual presence of each other. But so far as the telepathic or astral psychic powers are concerned, the mere extension of space does not change the principle.

The student who has developed his power of psychic induction in the phases mentioned in the preceding chapter, may begin to experiment and practice psychic induction at long-range, if he so wishes. That is to say, instead of causing psychic induction in the minds of persons actually in his presence and sight, he may produce similar results in persons out of his sight and presence. The person may be brought into presence and psychic contact, for all practical purposes, by using the visualizing powers for the purpose of bringing him into the en rapport condition. That is to say, by using the imagination to bring into the mind a strong clear picture of the other person, you may induce an en rapport condition in which he will be practically in the same psychic relation to you as if he were actually before you. Of course, if he is sufficiently well informed regarding occult matters, he may shut you out by drawing a psychic circle around himself which you cannot penetrate, or by surrounding himself with psychic armor or atmosphere such as I have already mentioned in preceding lessons. But as he will not likely know anything of this, the average person may be reached in the manner just mentioned.

Or again, you may establish en rapport conditions by psychometric methods, by holding to your forehead an article which has been in the other person's possession for some time; an article worn by him; a piece of his hair; etc. Or, again, you may use the crystal to bring up his astral vision before you. Or, again, you may erect an "astral tube" such as I will mention a little further on in this chapter, and thus establish a strong en rapport condition.

Having established the en rapport condition with the other person, and having thus practically brought him into your presence, psychically speaking, you may proceed to send him commands or demands, just as you did in the phase of personal psychic influence previously mentioned. You act precisely as if the other person were present before you, and state your commands or demands to him just as you would were he seated or standing in your presence. This is the keynote of the whole thing; the rest is simply an elaboration and stating of details of methods, etc. With the correct principle once established, you may apply the same according to your own wishes and discretion.

This phase of distant psychic influence is at the bottom of all the wonderful tales, stories and legends of supernatural powers, witchcraft, sorcery, etc., with which the pages of history are filled. There is of course always to be found much distortion and exaggeration in these legends and tales, but they have truth at the bottom of them. In this connection, let me call your attention to a very important psychic principle involved. I have told you that by denying the power of any person over you, you practically neutralize his psychic power—the stronger and more positive your belief in your immunity, and your denial of his power over you, the more do you rob him of any such power. The average person, not knowing this, is more or less passive to psychic influences of other persons, and may be affected by them to a greater or less extent, depending upon the psychic development of the person seeking to influence him. At the extreme of the sensitive pole of psychic influence, we find those persons who believe firmly that the other person has power over them, and who are more or less afraid of him. This belief and fear acts to make them particularly sensitive and impressionable, and easily affected by his psychic induction. This is the reason that the so-called witches and sorcerers and others of evil repute have been able to acquire such a power over their victims, and to cause so much trouble. The secret is that the victims believed in the power of the other person, and feared their power. The greater the belief in, and fear of, the power of the person, the greater the susceptibility to his influence; the greater the sense of power of neutralizing the power, and the disbelief in his power to affect them, the greater the degree of immunity: this is the rule!

Accordingly we find that persons in various stages of the history of the world have been affected by the influences of witches, sorcerers, and other unprincipled persons. In most cases these so-called witches and sorcerers themselves were under the delusion that they were assisted by the devil or some other supernatural being. They did not realize that they were simply using perfectly natural methods, and employing perfectly natural forces. For that matter, you must remember that magnetism and electricity, in ancient days, were considered as supernatural forces in some way connected with demonic powers.

Studying the history of witchcraft, sorcery, black-magic, and the like, you will find that the devotees thereof usually employed some psychometric method. In other cases they would mould little figures of clay, or of wax, in the general shape and appearance of the person whom they wished to affect. It was thought that these little figures were endowed with some supernatural powers or attributes, but of course this was mere superstition. The whole power of these little figures arose from the fact that they aided the imagination of the spell-worker in forming a mental image of the person sought to be influenced; and thus established a strong en rapport condition. Added to this, you must remember that the fear and belief of the public greatly aided the spell-worker and increased his power and influence over these poor persons.

I will give you a typical case, taken from an old German book, which thoroughly illustrates the principles involved in cases of this kind. Understand this case, and you will have the secret and working principle of them all. The story is told by an eminent German physician of the last century. He relates that he was consulted by one of his patients, a wealthy farmer living near by. The farmer complained that he was disturbed every night by strange noises which sounded like someone pounding iron. The disturbances occurred between the hours of ten o'clock and midnight, each and every night. The physician asked him if he suspected anyone of causing the strange trouble. The farmer answered that he suspected an old enemy of his, an old village blacksmith living several miles away from his farm. It appears that an old long-standing feud between them had broken out afresh, and that the blacksmith had made threats of employing his "hex" (witchcraft) powers on the old farmer. The blacksmith was reputed to be a sort of "hex" or male-witch, and the farmer believed in his diabolic powers and was very much in fear of them. So you see the ideal condition for psychic receptivity was present.

The physician called on the blacksmith, and taking him by surprise, gazing sternly into his eyes and asked him: "What do you do every night between ten and twelve o'clock?" The blacksmith, frightened and disturbed, stammered out: "I hammer a bar of iron every night at that time, and all the while I think intently of a bad neighbor of mine who once cheated me out of some money; and I 'will' at the same time that the noise will disturb his rest, until he will pay me back my money to get peace and quiet." The physician bade him to desist from his evil practices, under threats of dire punishment; and then went to the farmer and made him straighten out the financial dispute between the two. Thereafter, there was no more trouble.

So you see in this case all the necessary elements were present. First there was the belief of the blacksmith in his own powers—this gave him self-confidence and psychic power. Then there was the belief and fear on the part of the farmer—this made him an easy subject, and very susceptible to psychic induction, etc. Then there was the action of the blacksmith beating the iron—this gave force and clearness to his visualization of the idea he wished to induce in the mind of the other. And, finally, there was his will employed in every stroke, going out in the direction of the concentrated wish and purpose of influencing the farmer. You see, then, that every psychic element was present. It was no wonder that the old farmer was disturbed.

Among the negroes of the South, in America; and among the Hawaiians; we find marked instances of this kind. The negro Voodoo men and women work black magic on those of their race who are superstitious and credulous, and who have a mortal fear of the Voodoo. You see the conditions obtained are much the same as in the case of the German case just cited. Travellers who have visited the countries in which there is a large negro population, have many interesting tales to recite of the terrible workings of these Voodoo black magicians. In some cases, sickness and even death is the result. But, mark you this! it is only those who believe in, and fear, the power of the Voodoos that are affected. In Hawaii, the Kahunas or native magicians are renowned for their power to cause sickness and death to those who have offended them; or to those who have offended some client of the Kahuna, and who have hired the latter to "pray" the enemy to sickness or death. The poor ignorant Hawaiians, believing implicitly in the power of the Kahunas, and being in deadly fear of them, are very susceptible to their psychic influence, and naturally fall easy victims, unless they buy of the Kahuna, or make peace with his client. White persons living in Hawaii are not affected by the Kahunas, for they do not believe in them, neither do they fear them. Unconsciously, but still strongly, they deny the power, and are immune. So, you see, the principle working out here, also. Once you have the master-key, you may unlock many doors of mystery which have heretofore been closed to you.

We do not have to fall back on cases of witchcraft, however, in order to illustrate this phase of the use of psychic influence for selfish ends. In Europe and America there are teachers of a low form of occultism who instruct their pupils in the art of producing induced mental states in the minds of others, for purposes of financial gain or other selfish ends. For instance, there is a Western teacher who instructs his pupils to induce desired mental states in prospective customers, or others whom they may wish to influence for selfish reasons. This teacher tells his pupils to: "Imagine your prospective customer, or other person, as seated in a chair before which you are standing. Make the imagined picture as strong as possible, for upon this depends your success. Then proceed to 'treat' this person just as if he were actually present. Concentrate your will upon him, and tell him what you expect to tell him when you meet him. Use all of the arguments that you can think of, and at the same time hold the thought that he must do as you say. Try to imagine him as complying with your wishes in every respect, for this imagining will tend to 'come true' when you really meet the person. This rule may be used, not only in the case of prospective customers, but also in the case of persons whom you wish to influence in any way whatsoever." Surely this is a case of employing psychic powers for selfish purposes, if anything is.

Again, in Europe and America, particularly in the latter country, we find many persons who have picked up a smattering of occult knowledge by means of some of the many healing cults and organizations which teach the power of thought over physical diseases. In the instruction along the lines of distant mental healing, the student is taught to visualize the patient as strongly and clearly as possible, and to then proceed to make statements of health and strength. The mind of the patient, and that of the healer, cooperate and in many cases work wonderful cures. As you will see in the last lesson of this course, there is great power in the mind to induce healthful vibrations in the mind of others, and the work is a good and worthy one. But, alas! as is so often the case, the good teaching is sometimes perverted, and applied for unworthy and selfish ends. Some of the persons who have picked up the principles of mental healing have discovered that the same power may be used in a bad as well as in a good direction. They accordingly, proceed to "treat" other persons with the object of persuading them to do things calculated to benefit the person using the psychic power. They seek to get these other persons under their psychic influence, and to then take advantage of them in some way or other.

I hope that it is practically unnecessary for me to warn my students against evil practices of this kind—I trust that I have not drawn any students of this class to me. In case, however, that some of you may have been, or may be in the future, tempted to use your psychic powers improperly, in this way, I wish to caution and warn you positively against so doing. Outside of the ordinary morality which should prevent you from taking advantage of another person in this way, I wish to say to you that anyone so misusing psychic or astral powers will inevitably bring down upon his head, sooner or later, certain occult astral forces which will prove disastrous to him. He will become involved in the web of his own making, and will suffer greatly. Never by any means allow yourself to be tempted into indulging in any of the practices of Black Magic, under any form of disguise. You will live to regret it if you do. Employ your powers, when you develop them, for the good of others; or at least, for purely scientific investigation and knowledge.

The scientific investigator of this phase of psychic influence, will wish to become acquainted with what the occultists call "the astral tube." In this phase of the phenomena, you manifest upon the astral plane, rather than upon the physical. The astral form of telepathy is manifested, rather than the ordinary form. While there are a number of technical points involved in the production of the astral tube, I shall endeavor to instruct you regarding its creation and use in as plain words as possible, omitting all reference to technical occult details which would only serve to distract your attention and confuse your mind. The advanced occult student will understand these omitted technicalities without being told of them; the others would not know what was meant by them, if mentioned, in the absence of a long stage of preparatory teaching. After all, the theory is not of so much importance to most of you as are the practical working principles. I ask your careful attention to what I have to say in this subject of the astral tube.

The Astral Tube is formed by the person forming in his imagination (i.e., on the astral plane by means of his imagination or visualizing powers), a tube or small tunnel between himself and the person whom he wishes to influence. He starts by picturing it in his mind a whirling vortex, similar to the whirling ring of smoke emitted from a "coughing" engine, and sometimes by a man smoking a cigar, about six inches to one foot in diameter. He must will the imagined vortex-ring to move forward as if it were actually boring a tunnel through the atmosphere. When the knack of producing this astral tube is acquired, it will be found that the visualized tunnel seems to vibrate with a peculiar intensity, and will seem to be composed of a substance far more subtle than air. Then, at the other end of this astral tube you must picture the other person, the one whom you wish to influence. The person will seem as if viewed through the wrong end of an opera-glass. When this condition is gained, there will be found to be a high degree of en rapport between yourself and the other person. The secret consists in the fact that you have really established a form of clairvoyance between yourself and the person. When you have induced this condition, proceed with your mental commands and pictures just as if you were in the presence of the person himself. That is the whole thing in a nutshell.

In order that you may have another viewpoint from which to consider the astral tube, or what corresponds to it, I wish to give you here a little quotation from another writer on the subject, who presents the matter from a somewhat more technical standpoint. Read this quotation in connection with my own description of the astral tube, and you will form a pretty complete and clear idea of the phenomenon. The writer mentioned says: "It is impossible here to give an exhaustive disquisition on astral physics; all I need say is that it is possible to make in the astral substance a definite connecting-line that shall act as a telegraph wire to convey vibrations by means of which all that is going on at the other end of it may be seen. Such a line is established, be it understood, not by a direct projection through space of astral matter, but by such action upon a line (or rather many lines) of particles of that substance as will render them capable of forming a conductor for vibrations of the character required. This preliminary action can be set up in two ways—either by the transmission of energy from particle to particle, until the line is formed, or by the use of a force from a higher plane which is capable of acting upon the whole line simultaneously. Of course this latter method implies far greater development, since it involves the knowledge of (and the power to use) forces of a considerably higher level.

"Even the simpler and purely astral operation is a difficult one to describe, though quite an easy one to perform. It may be said to partake somewhat of the nature of the magnetization of a bar of steel; for it consists in what we might call the polarization, by an effort of the human will, of a number of astral atoms reaching from the operator to the scene which he wishes to observe. All the atoms thus affected are held for the time being with their axes rigidly parallel to one another, so that they form a kind of temporary tube along which the clairvoyant may look. This method has the disadvantage that the telegraph line is liable to disarrangement or even destruction by any sufficiently strong astral current which happens to cross its path; but if the original creative effort were fairly definite, this would be a contingency of only infrequent occurrence. The view of a distant scene obtained by means of this 'astral current' is in many ways not unlike that seen through a telescope. Human figures usually appear very small, like those on a distant stage, but in spite of their diminutive size they are as clear as though they were close by. Sometimes it is possible by this means to hear what is said as well as to see what is done; but as in the majority of cases this does not happen, we must consider it rather as the manifestation of an additional power than as a necessary corollary of the faculty of sight."

I would feel that I had not done my whole duty to the student, or reader of this book, were I to conclude this chapter without pointing out a means of protection against the use of this phase of psychic influence against them on the part of some unscrupulous person; or for that matter, against the meddling influence of any person whatsoever, for any purpose whatsoever, without one's permission and consent. Therefore, I wish now to point out the general principles of self-protection or defense against this class of psychic influence.

In the first place, you must, of course, refuse to admit to your mind any feeling of fear regarding the influence of other persons—for that is the open door to their influence, as I have pointed out to you. If you have been, or are fearful of any persons psychic influence, you must get to work and drive out that feeling by positive and vigorous denials. The denial, you remember, is the positive neutralizer of the psychic influence of another person, providing you make it in full belief of its truth. You must take the position (which is a true one) that you are immune to the psychic attack or influence. You should say, mentally, "I deny to any person the power to influence me psychically without my consent; I am positive to all such influences, and they are negative to me; I neutralize them by this denial!"

If you feel sudden impulses to act in some way which you have not thought of doing, or toward which you have had an aversion, pause a moment and say, mentally, "If this is an outside influence, I deny its power over me; I deny it, and send it back to its sender, to his defeat and confusion." You will then experience a feeling of relief and freedom. In such cases you may frequently be approached later on by the person who would have been most benefitted by your action; he will appear surprised when you "turn him down," and will act in a confused way. He may not have consciously tried to influence you, but may have merely been wishing strongly that you would do as he desired.

It should encourage you to know that it requires much less force to repel and neutralize psychic influence of this kind, than is required to send forth the power; an ounce of denial and protection overcomes a pound of psychic attacking power. Nature gives you the means of protection, and gives you "the best end of the stick," and it is your own fault if you do not effectively use it. A word to the wise is sufficient.

LESSON - XIX

LAWS OF PSYCHIC ATTRACTION

The third phase of Psychic Influence is that which may be called Indirect Psychic Influence, in which psychic induction is manifested in the minds of other persons coming in contact with the thought vibrations of the person manifesting them, although no deliberate attempt is made to influence the mind of any particular person or persons. Closely connected with and involved in this phase of psychic influence, is that which is called the Psychic Law of Attraction. So closely are these two connected that I shall consider them together in this lesson.

The fundamental principle of this phase of psychic influence is the well-known psychic fact that mental and emotional states not only inducesimilar vibrations in those who are similar attuned on the psychic vibratory scale, but also tend to attract and draw to the person other persons who are vibrating along similar lines, and also tend to repel those who are vibrating in an opposing note or scale of psychic vibration.

In the preceding lessons I have shown you how by induction we tend to arouse in others mental and emotional states similar to our own. But there is a law in effect here, which must be noted if you wish to thoroughly understand this phase of psychic influences. Omitting all technical explanations, and getting right down to the heart of the phenomenon, I would say that the general principle is this: Psychic induction is difficult in proportion to the opposing quality of the characteristic mental and emotional states of the person affected; and easy in proportion to the harmonious quality thereof. That is to say, in plain words, that if a person's habitual thought and emotions are along the same lines that you are trying to induce in him, you will find it easy to induce the same in him; if, on the contrary, they are of an opposing nature, then you will find it difficult to so influence him. The many degrees of agreement and difference in the psychic vibrations of persons constitute a scale of comparative response to any particular form of mental or emotional vibrations.

It is hard to change the spots of a leopard, or the skin of an Ethiopian, as we are told on ancient authority. It is almost as difficult to change the characteristic mental and emotional states of a person by psychic induction, except after long and repeated efforts. On the contrary, let a person have certain characteristic mental and emotional habits, then these may be aroused in them with the greatest ease by means of psychic induction. For instance, if a person is characteristically and habitually peaceful, mild and calm, it will be very difficult to arouse in him by psychic induction the vibrations of anger, fight and excitement. On the other hand, if the other person is combative, fierce and easily excited to wrath, it is the easiest possible thing to arouse these feelings in him by psychic induction. So much for ordinary psychic induction; let us now consider indirect psychic induction, in which the same principle operates.

In indirect psychic induction, that is to say in cases in which psychic vibrations are aroused by induction without deliberate attempt or design to influence any particular person or persons, there is noted the manifestation of a peculiar law of attraction and repulsion along psychic lines. This psychic law operates in the direction of attracting to oneself other persons who, actively or passively, vibrate on the same note, or on some note or notes in general harmony therewith. In the same, way, the law causes you to repel other persons who vibrate on a note or notes in general inharmony or discord to yourself. So, in short, we go through life attracting or repelling, psychically, others in harmonious or inharmonious psychic relation to us, respectively. An understanding of this law and its workings will throw light upon many things in your life which you have not understood previously.

You of course understand that you are constantly radiating currents of psychic vibrations, some of which flow out to great distances from you, and affect others often far removed from you in space. But you may not also know that on the astral plane there is manifesting a similar sequence of cause and effect. A strong emotional vibration, or a strong desire or will, tends to manifest on the astral plane by attracting or repelling others in psychic harmony or inharmony with you. This phenomenon is not so common as is that of ordinary thought vibrations from brain to brain, but it is far more common that is generally supposed. It is particularly marked in cases of men of strong desire and will, and strong creative imagination. These vibrations awakening response in the minds of those in harmony with them, tend to draw to one those other persons whose general character will fit in with the desires and ideas of the first person, or to repel those who are not harmonious therewith. This explains the peculiar phenomenon of strong men in business, politics and other walks of life, drawing and attracting to them other men who will fit in with their general plans and aims.

This law works two ways. Not only do you draw such persons to you as will fit in with your plans and purposes, but you are attracted to them by the same law. Not only this, but you will find that through the peculiar workings of this law even things and circumstances, as well as persons, will seem to be moulded by your strong desires and ideas, providing your psychic vibrations are sufficiently strong and clear. Have you never noticed how a strong, resourceful magnetic man will seem to actually draw to him the persons, things and circumstances that he needs to carry out and manifest his plans and designs. To many, not understanding this great law, these things have seemed positively uncanny and mysterious. But, now-a-days, the big men of business and politics are beginning to understand these psychic laws, and to apply them deliberately and with purpose.

Some of the great leaders in the business world, and in politics, are known to deliberately start into operation strong psychic vibrations, and to send out strong psychic currents of attraction, by the methods that I have already explained to you. They, of course, are filled with a more than ordinary degree of desire and will and, in the second place, they create very strong and clear mental pictures of their plans working out successfully to a finish; then concentrate strongly on the thing; and lo! the effect is felt by all hands and on all sides. They "treat the public" (to use the term favored by some of the metaphysical cults of the day) by holding the mental picture of that which they strongly desire to come to pass, and by concentrating their thought and will strongly upon it.

A favorite mental picture of some of these men (who have been instructed by teachers of occultism), is that of themselves as the centre of a great psychic whirlpool, drawing to themselves the persons, things and circumstances calculated to bring success and realization to them. Others picture their thought-vibrations flowing from them like the rings in a pond into which a stone had been dropped, influencing a constantly widening circle of other persons; then they picture the persons being drawn to them in the manner just mentioned. They persist in this practice day after day, week after week, month after month, year after year—is it any wonder that they draw to themselves that which they desire?

Other persons of lesser caliber take similar advantage of the law in the same way, but on a smaller scale. In every community there are certain persons who seem to draw to themselves the patronage and custom of the community, in some peculiar way. In most cases this may be traced back to some form of psychic influence. I do not mean that these persons consciously and deliberately set these forces into operation. On the contrary, many of them do so more or less unconsciously, and without a knowledge of the underlying psychic principles involved. Such persons have stumbled on a portion of the psychic laws, and have used them more or less unconsciously and without understanding the real reason of the happening. They found out that certain mental states and certain mental pictures tended to produce certain results—that they "worked out"—and so they continued them. Some of these men think of the whole thing as something supernatural, and get to believe that they are being helped by some supernatural power; whereas, they are simply operating under a universal psychic law of cause and effect.

In America a number of teachers and writers have devoted much attention to this phase of the general subject of psychic influence. Cults have been formed upon this general basis, the main idea of their followers being that of attracting financial and other success by means of this phase of psychic force. One of the leading writers along this line, says: "An individual who has cultivated the faculty of concentration, and has acquired the art of creating sharp, clear, strong, mental images, and who when engaged in an undertaking will so charge his mind with the idea of success, will be bound to become an attracting centre. And if such an individual will keep his mental picture ever in his mind, even though it be in the background of his mind, when he is attending to the details and planning of his affairs—if he will give his mental picture a prominent place in his mental gallery, taking a frequent glance at it, and using his will upon it to create new scenes of actual success, he will create for himself a centre of radiating thought that will surely be felt by those coming within its field of influence.

"Such a man frequently 'sees people as coming to him and his enterprises, and as falling in line with his plans. He mentally 'sees' money flowing in to him, and all of his plans working out right. In short, he mentally imagines each step of his plans a little ahead of the time for their execution, and he concentrates forcibly and earnestly upon them. It is astonishing to witness how events, people, circumstances, and things seem to move in place in actual life as if urged by some mighty power to serve to materialize the conditions so imaged in the mind of the man. But, understand, there must be active mental effort behind the imaging. Day dreamers do not materialize thought—they merely dissipate energy. The man who converts thought in activity and material being throws energy into the task, and puts forth his willpower through the pictured image. Without the rays of the will there will be no picture projected, no matter how beautifully the imagination has projected it. Thought pictured in mental images, and then vitalized by the force of the desire, and will, tend to objectify themselves into material being."

The student will be interested in reading and hearing the various theories and explanations given by different writers and teachers to account for the phenomena of psychic influence. Once he has grasped the real scientific principles involved, he will be able to see the same in operation in all of the cases cited by the different teachers and writers, and will find that this fundamental principle fully explains and accounts for all of these cases, no matter how puzzling they may seem, or how mysterious they may be claimed to be by those mentioning them. Truth is very simple when we brush away the fantastic dressings which have been placed around it by those who have lacked knowledge of the true fundamental principles.

We see this same law or principle operating in very many different ways from those previously mentioned. For instance, we frequently find cases in which one person has a strong desire for a certain kind of assistance in his business or other work. He has almost given up hope of finding the right kind of person, for those whom he has tried have failed to measure up the requirements of the situation. If he will (and he sometimes does) follow the general plan just mentioned, he will set into operation the psychic forces which will attract that person to him, and him to that person. In some peculiar way, the two will be thrown together, and the combination will work out to the best advantage of both. In these cases, each person is seeking the other, and the psychic forces of attraction, once set into operation, serve to bring them together.

In like manner, one often draws to himself certain knowledge and information that he requires or is desirous of gaining. But, and you must always remember this, no miracle is worked, for it is simply a matter of the working out of natural laws of cause and effect—attraction and response to attraction—on the psychic or astral plane. Such a person will accidently (!) run across some other person who will be led to give him the key to the knowledge he seeks. Perhaps a book may be mentioned, or some reference to some writer be made. If the hint is followed up, the desired information comes to light. Many persons have had the psychic experience of being led to some book store and induced to examine a particular shelf of books, whereupon a particular book presents itself which changes the whole course of the person's life. Or, perhaps, one will pick up a newspaper apparently at random, and without purpose; and therein will find some information, or at least a hint in the direction where the information may be found. When one accustoms himself to the workings of psychic forces, these things soon become accepted as a matter of course, and cease to arouse wonder or surprise. The workings of the Psychic Law of Attraction is seen to be as natural and invariable as the law of gravitation, or magnetic attraction, once one has mastered its principles, and learned the methods of its application. Surely such a wonderful law is well worth study, attention, investigation, and mastery, isn't it?

A writer along the lines of Mental Science, which is really based on the principles which have been stated in this book, has the following to say regarding his system: "Wonderful results arise by reason of what has been called 'The Law of Attraction,' by the workings of which each person is continually drawing to himself the people, things, objects, and even circumstances in harmony and accord with his prevailing mental states. Like attracts like, and the mental states determine that which one draws to himself. If you are not satisfied with what is coming to you, start to work and change your mental attitudes and mental states, and you will see a change gradually setting in, and then the things that you want will begin to come your way. * * * A most important fact about the effect of mental vibrations upon people lies in the principle that one is more affected by vibrations in harmony with his own accustomed feelings and mental states, than by those of an opposite nature. A man who is full of evil schemes, and selfish aims, is more apt to be caught up by similar vibrations than one who lives above that plane of thought. He is more easily tempted by evil suggestions and influences, than one to whom these things are abhorrent. And the same is true on every plane. A man whose mental attitude is one of confidence and fearlessness, is not apt to be affected by vibrations of a negative, pessimistic, gloomy nature, and vice versa. Therefore, if you wish to receive the vibrations of the thoughts and feelings of others, you must place yourself in a mental attitude corresponding with those vibrations which you wish to receive. And if you wish to avoid vibrations of a certain kind, the best way is to rise above them in your own mind, and to cultivate the mental states opposite them. The positive always overcomes the negative—and optimistic mental states are always positive to pessimistic mental states."

Another writer on, and practitioner of Mental Science, in America, several years ago, explained her theory and practice by means of the term "corelation of thoughts and things." She held that when one thought positively, clearly and forcibly of a thing, he "related" himself to that thing, and tended to attract it to him, and to be attracted toward it. She held that true wisdom consists in so managing our thoughts that we shall relate ourselves only to those things which we know to be desirable and beneficial to ourselves, and to avoid thinking of those which are harmful and detrimental to us. The student of this book will see how this practical Mental Scientist was really using the same principles that we have examined and become acquainted within this book, although she called them by another name, and explained them by another theory. At the bottom of all the teachings and theories you will always find the one same basic principle and universal law.

The advanced student of occultism knows that each and every one of us is really a creator of his own circumstances, environment and conditions, to a great extent. Each of us is able to so modify our mental activities as to bring about such changes in our environment and surroundings as to actually re-create them. The things accomplished by successful men are really but materializations of that which they have previously held in their mental vision. Everything is first created on the psychic plane, and then manifested in the physical world. All the great works of man, the great bridges, great buildings, tunnels, machinery, cities, railroads, canals, works of art, musical compositions, etc., first existed in the mind of their creators, and were then afterward materialized in physical form and shape. And, so you see we are proceeding with our work of mental creations whenever we think and make mental images. This, however, is no new teaching. It is as old as the race of mankind. Over twenty-five hundred years ago, Buddha said to his disciples: "All that we are is the result of what we have thought; it is founded on our thoughts; it is made up of our thoughts."

I would be telling you but half the story did I not warn you that strong Fear may play the part ordinarily filled by Desire in the production of the psychic phenomena of materialization of mental pictures. Strange as it may appear at first, a strong fear that a thing will come to pass will act much the same as a strong desire that the happening will occur. Consequently, many persons by continually dwelling upon the thing that they fear may happen to them, actually attract that thing to them, just as if they had actually desired and wished for it. I cannot go into occult technicalities in explaining this strange fact; but the gist of the secret may be said to consist in the fact that the person clearly and vividly pictures in his mind the thing that he fears may happen to him. He thus creates a strong mental-picture or image of it, which sets into forces the attractive power of psychic influence and draws the feared thing into material reality. As Job said: "The thing that I feared hath come upon me." The moral of this is, of course, that persons should learn to stamp out fear and mental images of things feared. Instead, they should make strong positive mental denials of the things that they may find themselves fearing. They should deny the reality of the feared thing, and assert positively their own superiority to the thing, and their power to overcome it.

A great religious cult has sprung into existence which makes a leading doctrine of this ability to materialize the things which one desires, and to deny out of existence undesirable things. Many persons who have witnessed the wonderful success of some of the followers of this cult or organization, have been puzzled to account for the same on scientific and rational grounds. A little understanding of fundamental occult and psychic principles, as given in these lessons, will show the "why and wherefore" of these strange and wonderful manifestations. In this connection you must remember that the combined thought of the thousands of persons composing this cult or organization undoubtedly gives additional psychic force to the mental affirmations and denials of the individual member thereof.

In past and present, and probably in future time, there have been many instances of magical procedures tending to bring about the results that we have herein seen to come about by reason of psychic influence, in some of its many phases. These magic procedures have usually been accompanied by incantations, ceremonies, strange rites, evocations, etc., which were supposed to have great virtue in bringing about desired results. But the true occultists now know that these ceremonies and rites were merely hopes to the imagination and aids to faith, and thus tended to bring about the psychic phenomena. There was no virtue in these ceremonies themselves, and the same results may be secured by simply following the procedure outlined in this book. The wonders of ancient magic have been reproduced by the modern occultists, without all the mumbo-jumbo of the past rites and ceremonies.

A gifted English writer upon the subject of the relation of mysticism and magic, sums up the gist of the principles of Magic as follows:

"The central doctrine of Magic may now be summed up thus:

"(1) That a supersensible and real cosmic medium exists, which interpenetrates, influences, and supports the tangible and apparent world, and is amenable to the categories both of meta-physics and of physics." [This of course is the astral plane, which is the container of the subtle form or framework of all that exists on the physical plane.]

"(2) That there is an established analogy and equilibrium between the real (and unseen) world, and the illusory manifestation that we call the world of sense." [By this of course is meant the correspondence and balance between the subtle form of things and the material manifestation thereof. Things created in the astral, tend to materialize on the physical plane. All creation proceeds from the astral to the physical.]

"(3) That this analogy may be discerned, and this equilibrium controlled, by the disciplined will of man, which thus becomes master of itself and of fate." [The essence of Will consists of strong desire accompanied by a clear mental picture of the thing desired, and held steady and firm by concentration.]

So you see by reference to the above very clear statement of the central doctrine of Magic, and my explanations thereof, that in these lessons you have been taught the very essence of the wonderful, mysterious ancient Magic, and its modern counterpart. As for the various rites and ceremonies, as I have said, these are mere symbols and aids to mental imaging and concentration. As an eminent occultist once said, "Ceremonies being but artificial methods of creating certain habits of the will, they cease to be necessary when these habits have become fixed." The master of occultism sees ceremonies, rites, and ritual as but the playthings of the kindergarten scholar—useful and important so far as they go, but serving merely to teach the scholar, sooner or later, that he may proceed without them.

In this chapter I have condensed enough information to fill a whole book. I trust that you will study it carefully, and not miss its main points.

LESSON - XX

PSYCHIC AND MAGNETIC HEALING

Probably no phase of psychic influence is more familiar to the average person of the Western world than is that of the healing of physical ills and conditions by means of psychic influence under one name or another. Great healing cults and organizations have been built up upon this basis, and the interest in the subject has taken on the form of a great popular movement.

As is natural in cases of this kind, there have been hundreds of theories advanced to account for the phenomena of psychic healing, and a still greater number of methods of treatments devised to carry out the principles of the theories. Ranging from the teaching of actual divine interposition and influence arising from certain forms of belief and practice, covering many intermediate stages, the theories even include a semi-materialistic hypothesis in which mind is considered as an attribute of matter, but having a magic influence over the forms of matter when properly applied. But it is worthy of note that no matter what the general or particular theory, or what the favored method of application, these healing schools or cults, as well as the independent practitioners, meet with a very fair degree of success and perform quite a number of cures.

Many of these Western advocates and practitioners of psychic healing practically hold that the whole system is of very recent discovery, and that it has nothing whatsoever to do with ordinary occult science. The occultists however are able to smile at these ideas and beliefs, for they not only recognize the general principles involved, but they also are aware that these principles, and their application, have been known to advanced occultists for thousands of years. I do not say this in any dispargement of the moderns schools of psychic healing, for I am in full sympathy with their great work; I merely mention the matter that the student may get the right historical perspective in considering this phase of psychic phenomena and influence.

So far as the methods of application are concerned, the true occultist recognizes that most of the methods and forms of treatment are but outward cloaks or disguises for the real psychic healing principle. The gist of the real methods is to be found in the principles of the application of psychic influence which I have presented to you in these lessons, viz: (1) Strong desire to make the cure; (2) clear mental image or picture of the desired condition as actually present in the patient at this time; and (3) concentration of the attention and mind of the healer, so as to bring to a focus to two preceding mental states. Here you have the real secret of psychic healing methods—the rest are all elaborations thereof, dressed up forms and ceremonies which affect the imagination, faith, belief and confidence of the patient, and thus make the healing process much easier. In fact, with the proper degree of faith and confidence on the part of the patient, there is but little need of a healer, for the patient may treat and cure himself. However, in most cases, the presence of the healer aids materially in arousing the fate and confidence of the patient, and hastens the cure.

Again, so far as the theories underlying the cures are concerned, occultists are able to reduce them all to a single working theory or principle, which includes all the rest. Brushing aside all technical details, and all attempts to trace back the healing process to the ultimate facts of the universe, I may say that the gist of the principle of all psychic healing is that of influencing the astral foundation of the various organs and parts, cells and centres, so as to make it proceed to manifest a more perfect physical counterpart. All psychic healing is really accomplished on the astral body first—then the physical body responds to the renewed activities of its astral counterpart. To get the real significance of this statement it is necessary for you to realize just what the astral body really is. This once grasped, the difficulties vanish, and you are able to form a clear conception of the entire matter and process.

The astral body is a precise counterpart of the physical body, its organs, its parts, its centres, and its cells. In fact, the astral body is the pattern upon which the physical body is materialized. The astral body is composed of an etheric substance of a very high rate of vibration. In one sense it may be considered as a very subtle form of matter—in another as a semi-materialized form of force or energy. It is finer and more subtle that the rarest vapors or gases known to science. And, yet, it has a strong degree of tenacity and cohesiveness that enables it to resist attacks from the material side of nature. As I have said, each organ, part, centre or cell, of the physical body has its astral pattern or basis. In fact, the physical body has been built up, in whole and in all of its parts, on the pattern and base of the astral body. Moreover, in case of impaired functioning of the physical organs or parts, and impaired activity of the physical body, its limbs, etc., if we can manage to arouse the activities of the astral body we may cause it to re-materialize or re-energize the physical body, and thus restore health and activity to it. If the liver, for instance, is not functioning properly, we proceed to start up the activities of the astral counterpart of that organ, to the end that the physical organ may be re-energized, and recreated in a measure. All true psychic healing work is performed on the astral plane, before it manifests on the physical.

At this point, I should also call your attention to the effect of "prana," or life energy, in some cases of healing. This prana is what Western healers mean when they speak of "human magnetism" in their healing work. So far from being an imaginary force, as claimed by the physical scientists and materialists, it is known to all occultists as an active principle of the human body, and as of great efficacy in the psychic treatment of disease. I shall mention the details of this form of treatment as we proceed—I mention it at this place merely to call your attention to the fact of its existence.

Before passing on to the consideration of other phases of the subject before us, I would like to call your attention to the fact that from the earliest days of history there have been recorded instances of some form of psychic healing. In the earlier days the psychic healing work was left entirely in the hands of the priesthood of the various religions prevailing in the several counties of the world. Claiming to have an exclusive divine sanction to perform healing work, these priests used various ceremonies, rites, incantations, etc., in order to obtain their results. In many cases these priests were ignorant of the real psychic forces invoked and set into operation; they merely practiced methods which had been found to work out effectively, and which had been handed down to them by their predecessors. In other cases, however, the priests undoubtedly were skilled occultists, and had a very full knowledge of the forces they were using; though, as the masses of the people were very ignorant it was impossible to acquaint them with these things so far above their understanding; and, consequently, the priests applied the healing forces under the disguise of their religious ceremonies and rites.

From time to time, however, as civilization progressed, there came into prominence persons who worked cures of physical ills by means of magical ceremonies and other similar methods, but who were outside of the priesthood. Some of these men undoubtedly had a very fair knowledge of the real secret of their cures, though they disguised them to suit the mental condition of their patients, and, also, probably for purposes of self glorification. In other cases, however, it is probable that these healers had merely stumbled across the fact that certain things said in a certain way tended to work cures; or that certain physical objects seemed to have therapeutic virtue. They did not realize that the whole healing virtue of their systems depended upon the strong idea in their own minds, coupled with the strong faith and confidence in the mind of the patient. And so the work went on.

In some of the oldest records of the human race, the scriptures of the various peoples, we find that "laying on of hands" was the favorite method employed by the holy men and priests, and other performing healing work. From the first there seems to have been an almost instinctive recognition on the part of man of the fact that there is a healing power in the touch of the hand. Even ignorant and savage mothers instinctively apply their hands to the hurt bodies of their children—a custom that has its counterpart in civilized races, by the way. The child is taught to expect physical relief from the application of the mother's hands, and its mind at once pictures relief. Not only is the mental picture created, but the desire and confidence is established in the minds of both persons. The same thing is true of all "laying on of hands," and thus are the principles of all psychic influence brought into play. But this is not all there is to it. In the first place, there is an actual transference of prana from the body of the healer to that of the patient, which serves to energize and revitalize the cells and centres of the body of the latter. In the second place, there is the effect upon the astral body of the patient, which tends to materialize better physical conditions. In the third place, there is that combination and union of the minds of the two persons, which gives extra force and power to psychic influence. Is it any wonder that cures take place under these circumstances?

In the modern revival of the almost lost art and science of psychic healing among the general public, there has been unusual stress laid upon the feature of "absent healing," in which the patient and the healer are not in each other's presence. To many this has seemed actually miraculous, and as a positive proof of divine interposition. But a little thought will show the student that such cures are not unknown in the pages of history, as a casual examination of the sacred books of almost any religion will show. Moreover, the student will see that to the effect of certain principles of psychic influence there needs but to be added the principles of telepathic communication, or, better still, the principles of astral communication by some phases of clairvoyance, to account for the entire phenomena of "absent healing."

Space is no barrier on the astral plane, as you have seen in the preceding chapters of this book. Once the en rapport condition is established between healer and patient, and the rest is simple—the astral body is induced to energize more actively, and as a result the physical manifestation is improved and normal functioning restored. Of course, all this is wonderful enough—all psychic phenomena is, for that matter; but, we see that we do not have to go outside of established occult laws, principles and facts in order to account for some of these modern miracles which have puzzled and perplexed so many good persons who have not known of the occult teachings, and who fear that the world is being turned upside down, and Nature's laws overturned by these "new fangled" ideas and methods.

Perhaps the most simple method of healing by psychic influence is that which is at the same time the oldest method, i.e., the "laying on of hands." This method was revived about twenty years ago in America and Europe by the new school of "magnetic healing" which sprung rapidly into public favor. The other schools of psychic healing, generally known as "mental healing," "spiritual healing," "divine healing," etc., generally frown upon the use of the hands in psychic healing, deeming it "too material," and too much allied to hypnotism, etc. But this view is quite bigoted and narrow, for this method has no relation to hypnotism, and, moreover, it gives the patient the benefit of the flow of prana from the healer, while at the same time producing the psychic effect on the astral body, as I have just mentioned.

I take the liberty of quoting here something on this subject from my little book entitled "The Human Aura." In the chapter of that book devoted to the consideration of the subject of "Auric Magnetism," I said: "In cases of magnetic healing, etc., the healer by an effort of his will (sometimes unconsciously applied) projects a supply of his pranic aura vibrations into the body of his patient, by way of the nervous system of the patient, and also by means of what may be called the induction of the aura itself. The mere presence of a person strongly charged with prana, is often enough to cause an overflow into the aura of other persons, with a resulting feeling of new strength and energy. By the use of the hands of the healer, a heightened effect is produced, by reason of certain properties inherent in the nervous system of both healer and patient. There is even a flow of etheric substance from the aura of the healer to that of the patient, in cases in which the vitality of the latter is very low. Many a healer has actually, and literally, pumped his life force and etheric substance into the body of his patient, when the latter was sinking into the weakness which precedes death, and has by so doing been able to bring him back to strength and life. This is practically akin to the transfusion of blood—except that it is upon the psychic plane instead of the physical."

But the true "magnetic healer" (call him by whatever name you wish) does not make this pranic treatment the all-in-all of his psychic treatment. On the contrary it is but the less subtle part, which leads up to the higher phases. While treating his patients by the laying on of hands, he, at the same time, strives to induce in the mind of the patient the mental image of restored health and physical strength; he pictures the diseased organ as restored to health and normal functioning; he sees the entire physiological machinery operating properly, the work of nutrition, assimilation, and excretion going on naturally and normally. By proper words of advice and encouragement he awakens hope and confidence in the mind of the patient, and thus obtains the co-operation of that mind in connection to his own mental efforts. The astral body responds to this treatment, and begins to energize the physical organs and cells into normal activity—and the journey toward health is begun.

[In the little book just mention, "The Human Aura," I gave some valuable information regarding the influence of colors in psychic healing, which I do not reproduce here as it is outside the scope and field of the present lessons. Those who may feel interested in the subject are respectfully referred to the little manual itself. It is sold for a nominal price by the publishers of the present work.]

In the form of psychic treatment which comes under the head of Suggestive Therapeutics, great insistence is laid upon the verbal suggestion to the patient, on the part of the healer. The patient is told that he will get well; that his organs will function normally; etc., etc. But the student of the present lessons will readily see that the only virtue in the spoken words consists in their power to evoke and induce the mental image of the desired condition in the mind of the patient. The mental picture thus evoked produces a corresponding effect in the astral body of the patient, and sets into operation the materialization of desired results. In addition, the words produce a strong mental picture in the mind of the healer himself, and thus give form and strength to his psychic vibrations which are being poured out toward the patient. This is really the secret of suggestive treatment.

The many cults of metaphysical healing, in America and Europe, lay great stress upon what they call "affirmations," which are but statements of the patient of his or her faith in the healing power of God, or of Mind, or Spirit, or Principle (different names are used). The patient naturally has confidence aroused, and as naturally begins to picture the desired condition; this in turn reacting upon the astral body, and this upon the physical body or organ. In addition, the healer's mind is also set to work in the same way, and sets into motion the healing psychic forces in the way just mentioned. You will notice that the same principle is always involved and set into operation and manifestation.

There is no particular virtue in the form of affirmation used by the healer or patient, except the important virtue of being able to arouse strong mental pictures of restored health, proper functioning, etc. There is of course this also: certain forms of affirmations or mental statements are better suited than others to the particular wants of certain persons. For instance, a very religious person will be aroused better by affirmations and statements filled with religious sentiments and ideas; while a person of a purely scientific turn of mind will receive more benefit from affirmations in which the precise physiological functions are specifically mentioned; while the person who is fond of mystery and strange ceremonies will be better served in the affirmations or statements taken in the form of some magical incantation, etc. The difference, however, lies in the mind of the patient, rather than in the words themselves. Words are merely invokers of ideas—symbols of ideas. In themselves, words are nothing—ideas are everything.

If you wish to treat yourself psychically for some physical disorder, or if you wish to do good to others in the same way, you have but to put into operation the general principles of psychic influence herein described. That is to say, you must first be filled with the strong desire and wish to make the cure; then you must make a strong mental image of the desired result, as actually present. (Do not think of it as "going to be;" instead say and think that it "is now!"); then concentrate the attention firmly and positively upon the idea. You may aid yourself and others by affirmations or auto-suggestions (words creating desired ideas and mental pictures) if you wish—you may get better results in this way. In this connection, let me remind you that the healing work in many cases consists largely in placing proper mental pictures in the mind of the patient, thereby displacing improper and harmful mental pictures of disease, etc., which have been given lodgment there before. Many persons are sick because of improper and harmful mental pictures that they have allowed to be placed there by the suggestions of others. Fear and dread of disease often acts to bring about the feared condition, for reasons that you can readily see.

And, now, finally for the work of "absent healing" by psychic influence. I can state this to you very simply; it is this: take what I have just told you regarding personal treatments, and combine it with what I have told you in previous lessons about "long distance psychic influence"—then you will have the whole thing. Here is a sample of an effective distant treatment; or "absent treatment," to use the popular term—it may be varied and enlarged up to fit individual cases:

Sit quietly in your own room, inducing a calm, peaceful mental attitude and state. Then (in the way already told you in this book) make a mental picture of the patient as sitting opposite to you, or lying down in front of you. If you have never seen the patient, make simply a mental image of a man, or a woman, as the case may be, and think of the figure as being the patient. The best practitioners of distant psychic healing produce such a strong mental image of the patient that they can often actually "feel" his or her presence. (This of course is the result of a simple form of clairvoyance.) Then make a strong mental picture of the condition that you wish to induce in the patient—the healthy physical condition of the organ, or part or body, as the case may be. See this condition as existing at the present time, and not as merely to come in the future. At the same time, you will do well to mentally speak to the patient, just as you would in case he or she were sitting before you in the physical body. Tell the patient just what you would in such case. Pour in the suggestions, or affirmations, or whatever you may wish to call them. In some cases in which an excellent en rapport condition is established, patients become aware of the treatment, and sometimes can almost see and feel the presence of the healer.

A prominent Mental Scientist, of America, instructs his pupils to consider each of the organs of the patient, or of themselves, as having a separate intelligence; and, therefore, to "speak up to it" as if it really understood what was being said to its organ-mind. I would say that such form of treatment would be calculated to bring about very good results, indeed. The principle of concentration and mental picturing would be invoked very strongly in such a case, and the astral counterpart of the organ should respond to such treatment quickly and effectively. It is an occult fact that there is mind in every organ and cell of the body, and if the same is awakened in the astral counterpart, it will respond to the command, suggestion, or direction. The writer in question evidently is well acquainted with this occult law, judging from his other writings, and has simply veiled his knowledge with this easily understood method of treatment which undoubtedly will "do the work," to use the American term.

Finally, no matter what may be the theory, or method, given in connection with psychic healing of any or all kinds, you will find the same general principles underlying it that have been presented over and over again in this book. In fact, many purely material and physical remedies owe their success to the fact that they appeal to the imagination of the patient, and also inspire confidence in him. Anything that will inspire confidence, faith and hope in the mind of a patient, and will bring to his mind strong mental pictures of restored health and normal functioning of his organs—that thing will make for health for him. So, there you have the whole theory and practice in a sentence!

* * * * *

I would remind the student that these are not lessons to be read but once and then laid aside. In order to get from them all that they contain for you, you will find it necessary to read them several times, with a reasonable interval between readings for the knowledge to sink into your mind. I feel sure that you will find with each reading that there are many points that you overlooked before. The lessons cover a wide field, with many little excursions into bye-paths and lanes of thought. I trust that the reading and study will make you not only a wiser person, but also a stronger and more efficient one. I thank you for your kind attention, and trust that we shall meet again in the future.